The Comparison Instinct

Why You Measure Your Financial Life Against People You'll Never Beat

Jordan Ellis

First edition, 2026

Published by Jordan Ellis

Contents

Foreword

Somewhere around the fourth book in this series, I noticed I'd started checking how the other books were doing against each other. Not against a target. Against each other — this one's first month against that one's first month. None of the numbers meant anything on their own. I made them mean something by lining them up next to a different book entirely, written by the same person, for the same reasons, and I felt genuinely better or worse depending on how the lineup came out that week.

That's a strange thing to notice while you're in the middle of writing about money psychology, and it's the reason this book exists. I'd spent years writing about lifestyle creep and the quiet architecture of control inside a marriage, and I'd never once turned that same attention on the plainest habit of all: the one where you can't just look at your own numbers. You have to look at someone else's first, and only then decide whether yours are good.

I don't think this habit is rare or shameful. I think it's closer to universal, and that's exactly why it's gone this long without a book of its own. Loss aversion has a name people recognize now. But the reflex that makes you check your former classmate's house against your own before you've finished admiring it still mostly goes by no name at all, which means it mostly goes unexamined, which means it keeps making decisions for people who never agreed to let it.

What convinced me to write this book wasn't one dramatic story. It was how ordinary the material turned out to be once I started asking people about it — a freelancer recalibrating her whole risk tolerance because a college roommate's start-up sold, a man in his fifties who could recite his brother's net worth to the dollar but not his own without checking. Nobody thought of this as a financial problem. Most didn't think of it as anything at all. It was just the water they swam in — a background hum of comparing that had run so long it had stopped registering as a choice.

This book is an attempt to turn that hum into a sound you can actually hear. A habit you can hear is a habit you can finally decide something about.

— Jordan Ellis

Introduction

You are not thinking about your own money right now. You're thinking about someone else's, and calling it thinking about yours.

It happens fast enough that you rarely catch it mid-motion. A former coworker mentions, almost in passing, that they've paid off their mortgage. A sibling buys a second property. A friend from college posts, without meaning to boast, a photo that makes clear they took the kind of vacation you've been telling yourself you can't afford this year. And in the half-second after any of these small, ordinary disclosures, something in you runs a calculation that has nothing to do with your actual bank balance, your actual goals, your actual life as it stood five minutes earlier. It asks a single question, fast and automatic: *where does that leave me.* Not where does that leave me relative to what I want. Relative to them.

This book is about that question — not the single moment it gets asked, but the fact that it gets asked constantly, quietly, underneath decisions you'd swear were entirely your own.

Whether to take a new job with more risk and more upside. Whether now is finally the time to invest more aggressively, or less. Whether the number you've been saving toward is actually the right number, or just the number that happened to match what somebody else seemed to be reaching for. Whether you're behind, on track, or ahead — a verdict you almost never render by looking straight at your own life, but by holding your own life up against someone else's and reading the gap.

Here is the book's master thesis, the one sentence worth carrying past every chapter that follows: **your financial decisions are shaped less by what you actually want than by an ongoing, mostly unconscious scoreboard against people you never agreed to compete with, and the scoreboard runs whether or not you ever look at it on purpose.** You did not choose most of the names on that scoreboard. You didn't sit down one day and decide that a former roommate's income, a sibling's house, a stranger's visible success would become the yardstick against which your own financial life gets measured. The scoreboard built itself, the way most instincts do, out of a nervous system that evolved to answer one question above almost all others — *how am I doing relative to the people around me* — long before money existed to be one of the things the question got asked about.

This is not a book about jealousy, exactly, though envy shows up in these pages more than once, honestly named rather than softened into something gentler. It's not a book about social media, exactly, though the mechanisms that make a stranger's curated life feel like a fair comparison point get real attention here too. And it is very specifically not a book about what you buy to look successful in front of other people — that's a different problem, a real one, and it belongs to a different book. This book is about something quieter and, in a strange way, more consequential: the comparisons nobody else ever sees. The ones that happen entirely inside your own head, that never produce a single visible purchase, and that still manage to move your actual financial decisions — how much risk you take, what you count as enough, when you decide to make a change — as surely as if someone had reached in and adjusted the dial themselves.

It's worth being precise about what this book is not covering, because the distinction matters and because getting it wrong would make this book redundant with ground already covered elsewhere in this series. There's a difference between spending money because you want other people to see it, and quietly recalibrating your entire sense of what's normal, adequate, or ambitious because of what you've noticed about other people's lives. The first is a purchase made for an audience. The second is a private, ongoing act of measurement that never needs an audience at all — it happens whether or not anyone else ever finds out, whether or not you ever spend a dollar differently as a direct, visible result. You can live in complete financial privacy, tell no one your balance, show no one your portfolio, and still spend a significant portion of your inner life quietly ranking yourself against people who have no idea they're being used as a measuring stick. That private, invisible ranking — not the purchase, not the display — is what this book is actually about.

It's also worth distinguishing this from a different pattern this series has already examined: the moment a single number anchors your judgment and distorts it — a first price you see, a first salary offer, a figure that gets stuck in your head and quietly recalibrates everything that comes after it. That's a real and well-documented distortion, and it happens once, or at least it happens as a discrete event you could, in principle, point to and name. What this book describes is different in kind, not just in degree. It isn't a single number lodging itself in your head on one occasion. It's a standing habit — a comparison engine that never fully switches off, running continuously against a rotating cast of people, recalibrating not just one judgment but your entire sense of what a good financial life looks like, moment by moment, for years. An anchor is a rock dropped once into still water. What this book describes is closer to a current — always moving, always pulling, present in water you've long since stopped noticing is moving at all.

Consider how differently this plays out for two people starting from the exact same financial position. Take a woman in her early thirties, a nurse, solidly middle-income, with a modest but genuinely healthy retirement account and no debt beyond a manageable car payment. By almost any external measure, she is doing well — ahead of national savings averages for her age, financially stable, on a reasonable trajectory toward a comfortable retirement. And take a second woman, same age, same income, same account balances, same trajectory, down to the dollar. The first woman spends her evenings scrolling past updates from a friend group that skews unusually affluent — a few early tech hires, a couple of dual-income households with no kids yet, one friend who married into real money — and she feels, most days, quietly, persistently behind, despite objectively excellent numbers. The second woman's closest comparison set is a group of coworkers on similar nursing salaries, most of them carrying more debt than she is, several of them further from retirement-ready than she is. She feels, most days, quietly ahead, on the exact same numbers. Nothing about either woman's actual financial position explains the gap in how each of them feels about it, or the different decisions each of them is likely to make from here — how aggressively to save, whether to take on more risk chasing a bigger number, whether to feel calm enough to make a patient, well-reasoned choice or anxious enough to make a rushed one. The only variable that changed was who they happened to be standing next to.

This is the part of the pattern that makes it so much harder to catch than most financial instincts covered elsewhere in this series: it doesn't feel like comparison from the inside. It feels like assessment. It feels like you're simply taking stock, using available information, forming a reasonable judgment about how your life is going — the same way you'd check a thermometer to know if you have a fever. But a thermometer measures against a fixed, universal, biologically meaningful baseline. Your financial comparison engine measures against whoever happens to be in view, which is never fixed, rarely representative, and almost never chosen with any real deliberation. You didn't select your comparison group the way a researcher selects a sample. It selected itself, out of whoever you happened to grow up around, went to school with, work alongside, or, increasingly, whoever an algorithm decided to put in front of you — and every one of those selection mechanisms is systematically biased toward people who look like they're doing better than you, for reasons this book will get into at length.

It's worth sitting for a moment with why this particular scoreboard is so hard to walk away from, even for people who can see it clearly and would tell you, honestly, that they wish they cared less about it. The scoreboard isn't really about money at all, underneath its financial costume. It's about a much older question every social animal has needed an answer to: where do I stand in the group, and is my standing secure. For nearly all of human history, that question had real, immediate stakes — a low-ranking member of a small, interdependent group faced genuine risk to food, safety, and survival, and the instinct to track relative standing constantly, automatically, without being asked, was not a character flaw. It was a competent, well-calibrated response to a genuinely dangerous world. Money, in the modern era, has become the primary unit that instinct now measures in, largely because money is unusually visible, unusually quantifiable, and unusually entangled with nearly every other marker of status a person might otherwise track. The instinct itself is not new. Only the currency it's counting has changed.

Why does this matter enough to earn its own book, distinct from everything else already covered in this series? Because comparison, unlike most of the patterns already named in these pages, doesn't just distort how you feel about your money. It actively drives what you do with it — often in ways that run directly against your own stated goals, your own risk tolerance, your own considered plan, overridden in real time by a feeling you couldn't fully explain if someone asked you to. You take on more investment risk than you'd otherwise choose, not because you've done new research or changed your view of the market, but because someone in your orbit made a fast return on something you didn't own, and staying where you were started to feel less like patience and more like falling behind. You set a savings goal that has almost nothing to do with your actual retirement needs and everything to do with a number you overheard, once, at a dinner table, that lodged itself somewhere and never left. You decide, almost without noticing the decision being made, that a stable but unglamorous path isn't good enough anymore, because somebody adjacent to your life took a riskier one and it happened, this time, to pay off spectacularly. Comparison, in other words, isn't a mood. It's a decision engine, quietly running underneath decisions you'd swear were made on the merits.

The mechanism underneath all of this has a long and well-documented history in psychology, and it's worth naming plainly here at the outset, because every chapter that follows will return to some version of it. Social comparison — the act of evaluating your own standing, abilities, and circumstances by measuring them against other people rather than against a fixed, external standard — is not a modern quirk produced by prosperity, or a symptom of a particular technology, or a personal failing you can simply decide to stop doing through sheer willpower. It is a well-studied, deeply wired feature of how human beings evaluate their own position in the world, present long before money, long before markets, long before anything resembling the financial systems this book will spend most of its time examining. What's changed over the long run isn't whether people compare — every society ever studied, across every era anthropology has documented, shows some version of status-tracking and relative standing mattering enormously to its members. What's changed is the size, visibility, and manipulability of the comparison pool available to any single person at any given moment, and how deeply that pool now reaches into decisions that used to be shielded from it almost entirely — what risk to take with savings built over decades, what number counts as "enough" for an entire life, how a family talks about money across a generation.

It's worth pausing here on something this book will keep returning to, because it changes how you should read everything that follows: comparison itself is not the villain of this book. A healthy, calibrated sense of where you stand relative to realistic peers can be genuinely useful information — it can catch complacency, motivate real effort, and provide a sanity check against a plan that's quietly drifted off course. The problem this book actually addresses isn't comparison as a category. It's comparison that has gone unexamined for so long that it operates entirely below the level of conscious choice — a scoreboard you never agreed to keep, updated by people you never selected, deciding outcomes you never consented to hand over. The goal of this book isn't to talk you out of ever comparing yourself to anyone again, which would be both impossible and, frankly, a worse outcome than the problem it claims to solve. The goal is to move the comparison instinct from the basement of your decision-making up into a room with a light on — where you can actually see it operating, evaluate whether a given comparison is even useful, and decide, on purpose, whether to let it drive.

It's worth naming, too, why this book focuses specifically on financial decisions rather than treating comparison as a purely emotional topic. Feelings about money matter, and this book takes them seriously throughout. But feelings alone rarely justify an entire volume in a series built around decision-shaping patterns. What earns comparison its place here is the demonstrable, repeated way it reroutes actual choices — how much risk to take, what to save toward, when to change jobs, how to split an inheritance — through a channel that was never designed to produce good financial judgment in the first place. A feeling that stays a feeling is one kind of problem. A feeling that quietly makes your decisions for you, without ever being invited to, is a different and more consequential one, and it's the second kind this book is built to address.

You'll meet nine versions of this pattern across the chapters ahead: the habit of measuring your whole life's trajectory against a shrinking circle of old friends; the way the very group you compare yourself to keeps quietly upgrading the moment you catch up to it; the specific mechanism by which someone else's lucky outcome recalibrates your own appetite for risk; the internalized, arbitrary milestones that convince you a stage of life has a "correct" bank balance attached to it; the scoreboard that runs inside families, sometimes for decades, between siblings who would never call it a scoreboard out loud; the strange, complacent relief of comparing downward instead of up, and what that relief quietly costs you; the specific sting of learning what a professional peer earns, and what it does to your sense of your own worth; the comparison set assembled for you, rather than by you, and how thoroughly unrepresentative it usually is; and finally, the comparison that was never fair to begin with — measuring your own progress against a life that ran on a different set of rules entirely, a different decade, a different economy, a different set of odds.

Each chapter in this book follows the same shape, deliberately, the same way every book in this series does: a scene that shows the pattern in its ordinary, undramatic form, sometimes a second scene to prove it isn't confined to one kind of life, a look at the real psychological mechanism producing it — grounded in real, named research rather than a plausible-sounding guess — an honest accounting of what the pattern actually costs, and a set of concrete overrides you can put to use immediately, none of which require an account, a product, or a strategy this book has any interest in selling you. You don't need to read the chapters in order, and you don't need to find yourself in all nine. Most readers will recognize themselves clearly in two or three, faintly in a few more, and barely at all in the rest — which is exactly how a book about a universal instinct should land, since the instinct is universal but the specific rooms it moves through are not.

It's also worth saying plainly what this book will ask of you, and what it won't. It will not ask you to move to a smaller house, quit a demanding but rewarding job, delete every account that ever makes you feel behind, or otherwise reorganize your entire life around eliminating comparison as a category. That kind of sweeping renunciation tends to produce its own quiet resentment, and in any case it isn't necessary. What this book will ask, chapter after chapter, is something narrower and more durable: that you learn to catch the comparison the moment it starts running, trace it back to where it actually came from, and ask, deliberately, whether it deserves the authority over your decisions it's currently been given by default. Most of the time, once you can see a comparison clearly enough to ask that question, the answer becomes obvious on its own.

One last thing worth saying before the chapters begin. You will not be able to stop comparing yourself to other people by the time you finish this book, and that was never the assignment. What you can do — what every chapter ahead is actually built to help you do — is notice the comparison the moment it starts running, ask whether the person on the other end of it is even a fair measure of anything that matters to your own life, and decide, deliberately, whether to let their number keep setting your terms. That's a smaller ask than "stop comparing." It's also, unlike that larger and mostly impossible goal, something you can actually start doing today.

To understand why this instinct runs as deep and as automatically as it does, we need to start further back than any specific friend group, sibling, or coworker. We need to start with what it meant, for nearly all of human history, to simply know where you stood.

Chapter 1 — The Trajectory Check

Why the Question Isn't "Am I Doing Well" But "Am I Doing Well Compared to Them"

Five people who used to eat lunch together in the same dining hall now eat lunch, when they eat it together at all, twice a year, and one of those lunches is always the one that matters. Not because anyone announces an agenda. Nobody brings a spreadsheet. But somewhere between the appetizer and the check, it happens anyway — a mention of a promotion, a new address, a kid's private school, a number dropped so casually it could almost pass for accidental, and by the time the coffee arrives, everyone at the table has quietly run the same calculation without a single one of them saying it out loud: *where do I rank at this table now.*

You drive home from that lunch and you cannot, for the life of you, remember what anyone actually talked about for most of the two hours. You remember the ranking. You remember it with the precision of someone reciting a batting average — who bought a house this year, who's still renting, who got the title bump, who mentioned, a little too breezily, that things have been "tight" lately in a tone that didn't quite match the car they arrived in. You built this ranking without meaning to, the same automatic way you'd notice if someone in the group had gotten a haircut. It just registered. It always registers. And once it's registered, it doesn't stay in the parking lot with the rest of the small talk. It comes home with you, and it starts quietly editing decisions you'll make in the weeks that follow — how urgently to push for that raise, whether the modest, steady plan you'd been content with an hour ago still feels like enough.

It shows up just as sharply outside any one dinner table. A man in his forties keeps, without ever writing it down anywhere, a running mental account of exactly four people: a brother, two college friends, and a former business partner who left to start something on his own. He couldn't tell you his own retirement balance to the thousand-dollar mark without opening an app. He could tell you, without hesitating, roughly where each of those four people stand relative to him, updated continuously from fragments — a car, a vacation photo, a comment made in passing at a wedding two years ago that he has apparently never stopped running calculations against. He isn't obsessive about it in any way that would look unusual from the outside. He'd tell you, if you asked, that he doesn't really think about money that much. He is, in a very real sense, telling the truth. He doesn't think about money. He thinks about the four people, and money is simply the unit the thinking happens in.

A third version of the same pattern, further from any single friend group: a woman who left a stable corporate job eight years ago to run her own small consultancy tracks her own progress almost entirely against a mental image of "where I'd probably be" had she stayed — an imagined, composite former self built from the actual trajectories of two colleagues who did stay, whose LinkedIn updates she's watched for years with an attention she'd be embarrassed to describe out loud. Some years her actual numbers beat the imagined trajectory easily. Other years, particularly slow ones for her business, the gap feels enormous, disqualifying, proof she made the wrong call — even though the imagined trajectory she's measuring against was never a real forecast, just two specific people's specific luck, stitched together into a phantom she now treats as the honest baseline her own life should have hit.

What connects all three of these is the same quiet substitution: none of them are actually asking "am I doing well." They're asking "am I doing well compared to them," and answering the second question as if it were the first, without ever noticing the swap happened at all.

What's actually happening

It helps to start with why the comparison feels so involuntary — why nobody at that dinner table sat down and decided to keep score, and why the ranking assembles itself anyway, whether or not a single person at the table would endorse it if you described it to them plainly beforehand. Understanding that involuntariness is the whole key to this chapter, because it explains why simply deciding to stop comparing rarely works on its own. The mechanism runs upstream of the decision to stop.

Social psychologist Leon Festinger's foundational 1954 theory of social comparison begins from a deceptively simple observation: in the absence of an objective, external standard for evaluating your own abilities and opinions, people evaluate themselves by comparing against other people instead. Money is one of the clearest possible illustrations of exactly this condition. There is no thermometer for “enough.” There is no universal, biologically fixed number that tells a given person, at a given age, in a given life, that their financial situation is objectively adequate. In the absence of that fixed standard, the mind reaches for the next best thing — other people, preferably people similar enough to feel like a fair comparison, close enough in age, background, and circumstance that the comparison feels informative rather than arbitrary. Festinger’s original research focused mostly on ability and opinion. Money turns out to be one of the domains where the mechanism he described runs hardest, precisely because it’s so numerically concrete and so persistently ambiguous about what number should count as success.

It’s worth being specific about what makes a dinner-table comparison different from, say, a comparison against a stranger with a similar job in a similar city. The five people at that table share not just a starting point but a continuous, ongoing relationship — they will see each other again, will hear more updates, will be measured against each other again at the next gathering and the one after that. This continuity is what converts an isolated moment of comparison into a genuine, standing scoreboard, because each new data point doesn't arrive in isolation. It arrives layered on top of every previous comparison, building a cumulative sense of relative standing that a one-off comparison against a stranger could never accumulate in the same way.

There's a second layer worth understanding, because it explains why this comparison keeps happening on a delay, running continuously between the actual meetings that trigger it. Festinger's later work, and the large body of research it produced, distinguishes between comparisons made for accurate self-assessment and comparisons driven by something closer to a competitive, evaluative need — a felt requirement to know not just where you stand, but whether you're winning. The dinner-table scene at the top of this chapter is the second kind. Nobody at that table needed accurate information to plan their retirement. What they were running was closer to a status check, and status checks, unlike genuine information-gathering, tend not to resolve once they're complete. They tend to generate a follow-up question — *what do I do about this* — that lingers long after the actual data has stopped being relevant.

A related and equally important mechanism comes from research on what's often called **reference group theory**, a framework with roots in the work of sociologist Robert K. Merton, describing how people don't compare themselves against the general population or some abstract average, but against a specific, usually small, self-selected group they treat as the meaningful measure of their own standing. Your reference group is rarely chosen deliberately. It's usually whoever happened to be nearby during a formative period — college, an early job, a hometown — and it tends to calcify early and persist for decades, long after your actual life has diverged wildly from theirs in circumstance, geography, and opportunity. The man tracking four specific people isn't comparing himself to a representative sample of anything. He's comparing himself to a reference group assembled almost entirely by accident, twenty years ago, that has continued to function as his mental yardstick purely out of habit, never once re-examined for whether it's still a fair or even sensible comparison for the life he's actually living now.

There's a third mechanism worth naming, because it explains why this kind of comparison so often runs on incomplete, distorted information without anyone involved noticing the distortion: psychologists studying **impression management**, building on sociologist Erving Goffman's foundational work on self-presentation, have long documented that people selectively reveal the flattering parts of their lives and withhold the rest, not necessarily out of dishonesty, but because everyone does it, in every social exchange, as a basic feature of how people manage how they're seen. The dinner table isn't an accurate sample of five people's actual finances. It's five curated highlight reels, delivered live, each person editing in real time, each listener treating the edited version as complete data. You are comparing your fully known, fully felt, worry-included financial life against everyone else's greatest-hits reel — a comparison that is, structurally, rigged against you before a single number gets mentioned, because you're the only person at the table with access to your own footnotes.

A fourth mechanism deserves real attention here, because it explains why trajectory comparisons in particular carry so much more emotional weight than a single snapshot comparison would: research on **self-discrepancy theory**, developed by psychologist E. Tory Higgins, describes the specific psychological discomfort produced when a person perceives a gap between their actual self and some standard they hold themselves against — whether an ideal they aspire to or an "ought" they feel obligated to meet. A trajectory comparison — where do I stand now, relative to where this specific group of people stands now, given that we all started from roughly the same place — activates exactly this kind of discrepancy, and it activates it more sharply than an isolated comparison would, because a shared starting point implies a shared standard was always available to be met. It's one thing to feel behind a stranger whose starting conditions you know nothing about. It's a much sharper discomfort to feel behind someone who sat in the same dorm room, ate the same dining hall food, started, by every visible measure, from the exact same place you did —

because the shared origin quietly converts "different life, different outcome" into "same test, worse score."

There's a final piece worth adding, because it explains why this pattern is so specifically hard to outgrow even as your actual life circumstances change: the reference group you formed early tends to keep its grip through sheer duration of habit, a pattern related to research on **anchoring and adjustment** within judgment and decision-making, most thoroughly documented by Daniel Kahneman and Amos Tversky. Once a comparison group has served as your mental yardstick for long enough, checking against them stops feeling like a choice and starts feeling like simply how you know things — the same way an anchored number keeps exerting pull on a judgment long after the original reason for anchoring to it has expired. The man in this chapter's second scene doesn't reconsider whether his four-person comparison group still makes sense for his current life. The question of whether to reconsider never even arises, because the habit of checking against them has been running so long it no longer registers as a decision that could be revisited at all.

It's worth adding one more layer, because it explains why a trajectory check so rarely gets resolved by a single reassuring data point the way a simple worry usually does: psychologists studying **rumination** — the tendency to return repeatedly to the same distressing thought without making forward progress on resolving it — have found that comparative, status-relevant worries are particularly prone to this looping quality, because there is no natural stopping point built into the question itself. A worry about a specific, solvable problem eventually resolves, one way or the other. A trajectory check doesn't resolve, because the comparison group keeps generating new updates indefinitely, which means the rumination it produces has, structurally, no finish line — only fresh material arriving at each subsequent dinner, wedding, or unplanned encounter, and each new fragment reopening a question the previous one never actually managed to close.

There's an seventh mechanism worth naming, because it explains why a trajectory check so rarely gets neutralized by simply reminding yourself that comparison is irrational: research on **dual-process models** of cognition, most widely popularized through Daniel Kahneman's distinction between fast, automatic thinking and slow, deliberate reasoning, describes how a fast, automatic evaluation can complete itself — registering as a felt verdict — well before the slower, more reasoned part of the mind has a chance to weigh in on whether the comparison was even fair. By the time you consciously remind yourself that your friend's house doesn't actually say anything about your own worth, the automatic system has usually already delivered its verdict and moved on, which is why intellectually knowing a comparison is unfair so rarely feels like enough to undo the sting it already produced.

There's also a generational layer worth naming here, because trajectory checks rarely start in adulthood — they tend to have roots much earlier, in the informal, unspoken ranking systems that already exist among school-age peer groups long before money is a factor at all. Research on childhood peer status and social comparison has documented that children as young as elementary-school age track relative standing among their peer group with real precision, long before they have any vocabulary for what they're doing. The five-person lunch table in this chapter's opening scene isn't a new comparison structure invented in adulthood. It's very often the same social architecture, the same ranked positions, simply re-skinned in adult financial terms — which is part of why the ranking can feel so immediate and so familiar, even though the specific numbers being ranked are entirely new.

What it costs you

The most direct cost is a decision-making process quietly hijacked by information that has almost nothing to do with your actual life. A trajectory comparison doesn't just make you feel behind or ahead. It changes what you do next — how urgently you push for a raise you don't actually need yet, whether you take on debt to match a lifestyle a peer seems to be living, whether you abandon a patient, well-considered financial plan because it suddenly feels too slow next to someone else's apparent pace. None of these decisions get evaluated on their own merits when a trajectory comparison is driving them. They get evaluated against a moving target assembled from other people's highlight reels, which means the decision itself is only ever as sound as the comparison producing it — and the comparison, as the mechanism section above should make clear, was never sound to begin with.

There's a compounding cost specific to trajectory comparisons that snapshot comparisons don't carry: because the comparison group shares a real, remembered starting point with you, every update from them doesn't just register as new information. It registers as evidence about a choice you made, once, at a fork in the road you can now never revisit — the job you didn't take, the city you didn't move to, the risk you didn't accept. This turns an ordinary, healthy financial life into something that can feel, on the bad days, like a referendum on a decision made a decade or two ago, one you have no actual way of rerunning to check whether the other path would truly have gone better. You're not just comparing outcomes. You're relitigating a choice that can't be relitigated, using evidence that was never designed to answer the question you're actually asking it.

There's a quieter, longer-running cost that shows up specifically in how trajectory comparisons distort your sense of time. A single comparison is a snapshot; a trajectory comparison, run repeatedly over years against the same small group, compounds into something closer to a permanent scoreboard, checked and rechecked at every wedding, every reunion, every unplanned run-in at an airport. This means the emotional weather of your financial life becomes tied not to your own actual progress — which, measured honestly, is very likely steady, or even strong — but to the timing and content of updates from four or five people you rarely see and don't actually control. You can have an objectively excellent year, financially, and still feel worse about it than an objectively mediocre year, purely because of what the comparison group happened to disclose during each respective stretch. Your own felt sense of how your life is going becomes hostage to other people's news cycle.

There's a final cost worth naming, and it's the one most likely to persist even after everything else in this chapter has been understood and internalized: trajectory comparison against an early reference group locks you, emotionally, into a version of your own potential that was calculated a very long time ago, under conditions that no longer apply to anyone at the table. The friend who seems to be pulling ahead may be running a business that will collapse in three years. The one who seems behind may be about to make a decision that changes everything. A trajectory comparison run at any single dinner is a comparison of unfinished stories, presented as if they were final scores — and treating an unfinished story as a final score is, on its own, enough to explain why this particular comparison habit produces so much unearned anxiety, and occasionally so much unearned complacency, for so little actual information gained.

There's a cost worth naming that's easy to miss because it doesn't show up as distress at all, at least not at first: a trajectory check run often enough over enough years can start to feel less like an occasional intrusion and more like a genuine source of identity, a habitual way of knowing who you are relative to the people who knew you first. This is a strange, quietly costly outcome, because it means the comparison group stops functioning as a measuring stick and starts functioning as something closer to a mirror — a person can lose track, after enough years of checking, of what their own sense of a good life actually looks like independent of the five people at that table, because the two have been fused together for so long that separating them again takes real, deliberate effort most people never think to make until something forces the question, a falling-out, a move, a friend group that simply drifts apart on its own.

There's a cost worth naming that shows up specifically in how often a trajectory check gets triggered by nothing more than the ordinary rhythm of adult social life — a wedding, a reunion, a holiday, a chance encounter at an airport. Because these triggering moments are largely outside your control, and because they tend to cluster around occasions that are otherwise meant to be celebratory or restful, the trajectory-check habit has an unusual capacity to contaminate exactly the parts of life meant to provide a break from ordinary striving. A reunion that should function as genuine reconnection becomes, instead, another data-gathering session for a scoreboard nobody at the table actually wanted to keep.

There's a cost worth naming that shows up specifically in how trajectory checks distort a person's willingness to make genuinely good decisions that happen to look, from the outside, like falling behind. Leaving a stable but limited job to retrain for a more meaningful career, taking a lower-paying position that offers real work-life balance during a season that calls for it, choosing to live in a lower-cost area to prioritize time over income — all of these can be sound, deliberate choices, and all of them will register, on a trajectory check against a comparison group that didn't make the same trade, as falling behind. The scoreboard has no column for the things a good decision actually bought you. It only has a column for the number, which means trajectory comparison systematically punishes exactly the kind of considered, values-driven choice a genuinely well-lived financial life often requires.

The overrides

Choose, deliberately, one or two people whose full financial picture you actually understand well enough to compare against fairly, and let them function as your primary reference point. A single fair, accurate comparison is worth more than a dozen distorted ones — the goal isn't to eliminate reference points entirely, but to replace a large, accidental, unverifiable group with a small, deliberately chosen, genuinely representative one.

Name the reference group out loud, on paper, once. Most people have never actually written down who's in their comparison set — it just runs, silently, in the background. Take five minutes and list the specific people you catch yourself measuring against. Seeing the list on paper does something the mental version never does: it makes visible how small, how accidental, and how outdated the group actually is, which is often enough on its own to loosen its grip.

Notice the specific bodily sensation that accompanies a trajectory check, and use it as an early warning signal. Most people report a recognizable physical marker — a tightening, a dropped stomach, a flush of heat — in the moment a comparison lands. Once you can identify that marker reliably, it becomes a genuinely useful alert, arriving faster than conscious thought and giving you an earlier opportunity to interrupt the calculation than waiting for the thought itself to fully form.

Ask, for each name on that list, whether their starting conditions actually matched yours. A shared dorm room or a shared first job creates the feeling of a shared starting line, but rarely the reality of one — different family financial support, different debt loads, different health, different luck at exactly the wrong or right moment. Where the starting conditions weren't actually equal, the comparison was never fair, and naming the specific ways they weren't equal is usually enough to drain a comparison of its sting.

Replace the trajectory check with a trajectory log of your own. Instead of measuring your progress against a moving, outside reference point, keep a private, dated record of your own numbers — savings, debt, income — checked against your own past self, six months or a year back. This doesn't eliminate comparison; it redirects it toward the only comparison that actually contains useful information about your own decisions: the you from before.

When a comparison-triggering update arrives — a new house, a promotion, a mention of a number — delay any resulting financial decision by at least a week. The urge to immediately recalibrate your own plan in response to someone else's news is almost always sharpest in the first hour and considerably weaker a week later, once the initial status jolt has faded and you can evaluate the decision on its own terms rather than as a reaction to someone else's timeline.

Practice narrating your own highlight reel honestly to yourself, in private, the way you'd actually tell it if pressed for the full version. For every flattering fragment you receive from someone else's life, remind yourself explicitly of the footnotes you're not seeing — the debt behind the house, the burnout behind the promotion, the version of the story that never makes it into a dinner-table update. You don't need to know their actual footnotes to remember, reliably, that footnotes exist.

A closing script, for the moment right after a comparison-triggering update lands: "That's information about their life, not a verdict on mine." Say it silently, right in the moment, before the calculation has a chance to run its full course. It won't make the instinct disappear. It gives you a half-second of daylight between the update and the decision it would otherwise make for you — and a half-second of daylight is usually enough.

Give the good decisions that look like falling behind their own explicit ledger. Keep a private, ongoing list of the deliberate trade-offs you've made — time, meaning, flexibility, health — that a trajectory check would never credit you for. Reviewing that ledger alongside the scoreboard, rather than instead of it, restores information the comparison habit systematically deletes.

Notice which specific update tends to trigger you most, and ask what it's actually about. For most people, one particular category — a house, a job title, a vacation, a child's school — carries disproportionately more weight than the others in a comparison group's updates. That specific category is usually pointing at something worth examining directly: a genuine, unmet goal of your own, a value you haven't fully honored, or simply an old insecurity that predates the friend group entirely and was only ever waiting for a convenient target.

Before a reunion, wedding, or similarly loaded gathering, decide in advance how much comparison you're willing to let the day cost you. Naming a limit ahead of time — "I'll notice it happening and let it go, rather than carry it home" —

gives you a pre-committed response to reach for in the moment, rather than improvising one while the automatic verdict is already running.

The rule to remember: a trajectory comparison measures your fully known life against someone else's greatest hits, using a shared starting point that was never actually as equal as it felt — which makes it one of the least fair comparisons available, and one of the hardest to stop running anyway.

Chapter 2 — The Reference Group Drift

Why the Bar You're Measuring Against Keeps Moving the Moment You Clear It

She remembers the exact number, because she picked it herself, years ago, sitting at a kitchen table with a legal pad and an honest sense of what would feel like enough: a hundred thousand dollars saved, no debt beyond the mortgage, a stable job. That was the finish line. She built it carefully, based on her own numbers, her own life, nobody else's. It felt, at the time, like a real answer to a real question — not a guess, not borrowed from anyone, hers.

She cleared it two years ago. She remembers that too, oddly less vividly than she remembers setting the original number — a bank balance she checked one ordinary Tuesday morning that finally, after years, read the way she'd once imagined it would. She expected the finish-line feeling. She got, instead, roughly eleven minutes of something like satisfaction before her attention, almost on its own, drifted toward a new set of people — no longer the coworkers and college friends whose lives had defined "enough" back when she set the original number, but a slightly different, slightly more affluent circle she'd been spending more time around since her income grew: a couple of new neighbors, a colleague she'd been promoted alongside, one person from a professional group whose casual mentions of a vacation home had started to register, lately, as a data point rather than small talk. Somewhere in the eleven minutes between checking the balance and closing the app, without a single deliberate decision, her sense of "enough" had already re-formed itself around this new group instead of the old one. The hundred thousand dollars was still real. It had simply stopped being the number that mattered.

The same drift shows up on a much longer clock in a different life. A man built his entire sense of financial adequacy, for the first fifteen years of his career, around the households he grew up around in a working-class neighborhood — steady paychecks, modest homes, retirement that meant, mostly, Social Security and whatever a pension could stretch to cover. By any honest measure against that original reference group, he is, at this point, doing remarkably well — ahead of nearly everyone he grew up around, by a wide margin. But somewhere in his thirties, a new career took him into rooms full of a very different kind of household, and his internal reference group quietly, gradually, followed him into those rooms too, without his ever consciously electing to replace one measuring stick with another. He now feels, most days, that he's merely keeping pace — sometimes falling slightly behind — using a comparison group he never deliberately chose, measuring himself against a bar that used to sit twenty feet lower and somehow migrated upward exactly in step with his own climb.

A third version, faster and more visible: a couple who set an ambitious savings goal early in their marriage, back when their combined income was modest and the number felt genuinely stretching, achieved that goal roughly on schedule — and felt, for a matter of weeks rather than years, something like real pride and relief, before quietly, almost without discussing it, setting a new goal nearly double the size of the original, justified in the moment by a vague, half-examined sense that "everyone at this stage" seems to be aiming higher than they'd originally planned. Neither of them could point to a specific person's number driving the new target. The bar had simply moved, the way it tends to, the moment the old one stopped being a stretch.

What's actually happening

It's worth naming directly why this chapter belongs in a book about comparison at all, since at first glance downward comparison might seem like the healthy, well-adjusted version of the instinct this book otherwise treats as a problem. The honest answer is that it's neither purely healthy nor purely harmful — it's a real, functioning tool that solves the immediate problem of distress at the cost of solving the underlying problem the distress was actually pointing to. A smoke alarm silenced by removing its battery stops the noise just as effectively as putting out the actual fire does. Only one of those two responses addresses what the alarm was for.

The mechanism running underneath all three of these scenes has a name in the psychological literature, and it explains something that pure willpower and pure discipline both consistently fail to override: reference groups aren't fixed. They drift, systematically, in a specific direction, as a person's own circumstances change — and the direction they drift in is almost always upward, rarely down, regardless of whether upward is actually a sensible target for that particular life.

The clearest research on this comes from work extending Festinger's original social comparison framework into what's often studied as **assimilation and contrast effects** in comparison — the finding, replicated across many studies, that when a comparison target feels close enough to identify with, people tend to *assimilate* toward that target's standard, treating it as the new normal to be matched, rather than *contrasting* against it as a distant, aspirational outlier they can dismiss as irrelevant to their own life. The woman who cleared her original savings goal didn't dismiss her new, slightly more affluent neighbors as living a different, unreachable kind of life. They felt close enough — same neighborhood now, same rough social tier — that their standard assimilated directly into her own sense of normal, replacing the old reference group almost instantly, with no deliberate decision required on her part at all.

It's worth being specific about the actual mechanics of the goalpost move, because the phrase "moving the goalposts" can make it sound like a deliberate act, when the drift this chapter describes is almost never deliberate at all. The new goal doesn't arrive as a conscious counter-proposal to the old one. It arrives as a felt sense — a vague, ambient impression that the old target was somehow too modest — long before any specific new number has even been consciously formed. By the time the new target does get named, out loud or on paper, the actual decision to abandon the old one has already happened, quietly, upstream of any deliberate choice, which is exactly why it so rarely feels like a choice at all when you look back on it.

There's a second, closely related mechanism worth naming: research on the **hedonic treadmill**, a concept most associated with psychologists Philip Brickman and Donald Campbell's foundational work on relative standards of well-being, and later extended significantly by researchers studying happiness and adaptation, describes how people adapt quickly to improvements in their circumstances, resetting their baseline expectation upward to match the new normal, which means a genuine gain in well-being from an improvement tends to fade far faster than most people predict it will. Applied specifically to financial reference groups, the same treadmill effect explains why crossing a savings goal produces satisfaction measured in minutes rather than years — the achievement gets absorbed into a new baseline almost immediately, and the search for the next comparison point, the next bar to measure against, resumes on its own, without requiring any conscious decision to keep striving.

A third mechanism deepens this further: economist Fred Hirsch's influential concept of **positional goods**, later extended in detail by economist Robert H. Frank's research on relative consumption and status, describes a category of goods and achievements whose value is inherently relative rather than absolute — their worth to a person depends not on some fixed, intrinsic standard, but specifically on how they compare to what others in a person's social orbit have. A savings target framed purely in absolute terms — a hundred thousand dollars, full stop — sounds fixed. But the *feeling* the number was actually built to produce, the feeling of having "enough," has always been positional underneath the absolute framing, tied not to the number itself but to what the number bought in social standing relative to a specific comparison group. Change the comparison group — through a new job, a new neighborhood, a promotion — and the same fixed number stops producing the feeling it was built to produce, even though the number itself hasn't moved an inch.

There's a fourth piece worth adding, because it explains why the drift tends to be so specifically invisible while it's happening: research on **habituation** within psychophysics and later extended broadly into judgment and decision research describes how repeated exposure to a stimulus reduces the intensity of the response it produces over time — the same underlying mechanism that makes a loud room feel quiet after twenty minutes inside it. Repeated exposure to a new social tier — new neighbors, new colleagues, a new professional circle — produces the same habituation with respect to what counts as an impressive or adequate financial life. The vacation-home mention that would have stunned the woman in this chapter's opening scene ten years ago barely registers as noteworthy now, not because vacation homes have become less remarkable in any objective sense, but because her exposure to people who own them has become routine enough to reset what she experiences as remarkable at all.

A fifth mechanism worth naming, and arguably the most important for understanding why this pattern feels so much like personal ambition rather than a comparison trap: social psychologists studying **relative deprivation**, a framework developed substantially by sociologist Robert K. Merton and later extended by W.G. Runciman, describe how a sense of being deprived or falling short is produced not by an absolute lack of resources, but by a felt gap between what a person has and what a relevant reference group appears to have. The man who grew up in a working-class neighborhood and now feels, incorrectly, that he's merely keeping pace isn't experiencing an absolute financial shortfall by any measure. He's experiencing relative deprivation, produced entirely by a reference group that quietly reassembled itself around his new professional circles — a textbook instance of the exact mechanism Merton's research was built to explain, running in a life that would, by any honest external accounting, be described as a genuine success story.

There's a sixth mechanism worth adding, because it explains why the drift specifically resists a person's own deliberate effort to hold a fixed standard in place: research on **social identity theory**, developed by psychologists Henri Tajfel and John Turner, describes how people define part of their own sense of self through the groups they belong to or aspire to belong to, and how moving into a new group — a new profession, a new neighborhood, a new social tier — creates real psychological pressure to adopt that group's norms as a condition of genuinely belonging to it. Once the man in this chapter's second scene began spending real time in rooms shaped by a different financial tier, some part of the pull toward adopting their standard of "enough" wasn't really about money at all. It was about belonging — a separate, equally powerful motive that money simply happened to be the visible unit of, which is part of why reasoning about the actual dollar figures alone rarely loosens the drift on its own.

There's an seventh mechanism worth adding, because it explains why the drift so rarely gets caught in the act rather than noticed only well after the fact: the recalibration described throughout this chapter tends to happen through many small, individually unremarkable exposures rather than one identifiable event, which means there is very often no single moment a person could point to and say "that's when my sense of enough changed." Researchers studying gradual attitude change describe this as a well-documented blind spot — people are considerably better at noticing a sudden shift in their own standards than a slow, incremental one, even when the incremental version produces a larger total change over time. The woman who cleared her original goal didn't experience a single moment of her standard shifting. She experienced a hundred small, forgettable exposures to a new social tier, none of which felt significant enough to flag on its own.

There's a eighth piece worth naming, specific to why couples experience this drift so asymmetrically: research on **differential exposure within households** — the simple, well-documented fact that partners in a relationship are rarely exposed to identical social and professional environments even while sharing a home and a budget — helps explain why one partner in a marriage can feel the drift pulling hard while the other barely notices it happening at all. The partner with more daily exposure to an upgraded social tier absorbs the new reference group first, and often carries it into the household's shared financial conversations well before the drift has been named, discussed, or agreed to by the partner experiencing it secondhand, if at all.

What it costs you

The most direct cost of reference group drift is that it makes "enough" permanently, structurally unreachable — not because your actual financial position keeps failing to improve, but because the standard against which you're measuring it keeps quietly relocating exactly as fast as you approach it. This produces a specific, exhausting kind of dissatisfaction that has nothing to do with real financial hardship and everything to do with a moving target you never consciously chose to keep chasing. People living inside this pattern often report, honestly, that they can't identify a single number that would finally feel like enough — not because they're greedy, but because the drift mechanism guarantees that whatever number they name today will have been replaced, silently, by the time they actually reach it.

There's a compounding cost specific to how this drift interacts with major financial decisions. A savings goal, a retirement target, a decision about how aggressively to invest — all of these depend on having a relatively stable sense of what you're actually saving toward. When the underlying reference group keeps drifting upward, these targets become unstable in a way that produces genuinely poor decision-making: taking on more investment risk than your actual timeline or temperament calls for, in pursuit of a number that will have moved again by the time you reach it; working longer hours or taking on more professional stress than a genuinely examined life would call for, chasing a standard of "enough" that was never actually fixed to begin with.

There's a quieter cost that shows up specifically in how this pattern erases the memory of real progress. The woman who cleared her original hundred-thousand-dollar goal experienced roughly eleven minutes of satisfaction before the goalpost relocated — which means, functionally, she has almost no lived memory of having achieved something she once worked years toward. The achievement is real. It happened. And the drift mechanism, left unexamined, guarantees that it will be experienced, in retrospect, as barely having happened at all, replaced almost instantly by whatever the new, higher bar demands instead. This is a genuine loss, not a minor one — the erosion of a person's own ability to register and feel their own real accomplishments, systematically undermined by a reference group that never holds still long enough to let an accomplishment be felt.

There's a final cost worth naming, and it belongs to relationships as much as to individual well-being: when a reference group drifts without either partner in a household consciously noticing or discussing it, couples can find themselves quietly, gradually recalibrating their shared sense of "enough" in ways neither of them ever actually agreed to — one partner more exposed to the drifting reference group than the other, pulling the household's shared standard upward while the second partner watches a goal they thought was settled quietly, unilaterally, get replaced. This produces a specific, hard-to-name friction in a marriage or partnership: a sense that the finish line keeps moving, attributed vaguely to "wanting more" or "never being satisfied," when the actual mechanism is far more specific and far more addressable than either partner usually realizes — a reference group that shifted, and was never renegotiated out loud.

There's a cost worth naming that touches how a household experiences its own genuine, hard-won financial security. Security, felt honestly, should register as a settling — a real, embodied sense that enough danger has been addressed that a person can exhale. Reference group drift interferes directly with that settling, because it guarantees the exhale never quite completes: just as the nervous system starts to register that a goal has been met, the goal relocates, and the settling resets before it ever finishes. Over years, this can produce a strange, hard-to-name state in otherwise financially secure people — a persistent, background hum of insufficiency that has no obvious external cause, because its actual cause isn't a lack of resources. It's a target that was never built to hold still long enough to be reached.

There's a cost worth naming that's specific to how the drift affects a person's relationship to risk. Because a drifted reference group tends to sit just slightly out of reach, it can produce a persistent, low-grade pressure to take on more investment or career risk than a person's actual goals would otherwise justify — not out of any considered strategy, but simply as a way of closing a gap that keeps regenerating itself no matter how it's addressed. This is a quieter, slower-burning version of the same dynamic covered in the chapter on envy-driven return-chasing, and the two often reinforce each other in the same life: a drifted reference group supplies the ongoing sense of falling short, and a single vivid peer success story supplies the specific trigger that finally acts on it.

There's a cost worth naming that compounds specifically over a working life rather than any single goal: because the drift mechanism guarantees that each cleared target gets replaced almost immediately by a higher one, the total number of hours, and the total accumulated stress, spent chasing "enough" tends to run considerably higher across a lifetime than the person doing the chasing would ever estimate if asked directly. Retirement gets delayed a year, then another, each delay justified by a freshly drifted standard rather than any actual change in what the original, honestly calculated retirement number required. The drift doesn't just cost a feeling of satisfaction. Left unexamined for decades, it can cost real years of a life that could otherwise have been spent differently, on the strength of a target that was, by the original honest math, already met.

The overrides

Write your "enough" number down with a date attached, and revisit the date before revisiting the number. When you notice the bar has moved, check first whether your actual life circumstances changed enough to justify a new target, or whether your comparison group simply changed. These are different situations requiring different responses, and conflating them is exactly how an unexamined drift keeps operating unchecked.

When you catch yourself recalibrating a financial goal upward, ask explicitly: who moved this bar? Name the specific new comparison group — new colleagues, new neighbors, a new social circle — driving the recalibration. A moved bar with a named cause is far easier to evaluate honestly than a vague, ambient sense that you should probably be aiming higher than you used to.

Deliberately revisit an old, cleared goal and sit with having actually achieved it, on purpose, before setting the next one. Take real time — an afternoon, a specific conversation with a partner, a written note to yourself — to register a past accomplishment fully before the drift mechanism quietly overwrites it. This won't stop the next goalpost from eventually moving. It ensures you actually get to feel the ones you've already cleared before that happens.

Periodically audit who's actually in your reference group, and ask whether they represent a life you're genuinely trying to build, or simply a life you've become proximate to. Proximity and aspiration are not the same thing, and reference group drift systematically confuses the two — treating whoever happens to be nearby as if their standard were automatically the one worth chasing, regardless of whether it actually reflects your own considered values.

For couples or households, name the reference group out loud together, at least once a year. Because drift happens gradually and asymmetrically, it's easy for a shared "enough" to quietly become one partner's "enough," imported without discussion. A brief, explicit conversation — who are we actually comparing ourselves to right now, and did we agree to that — catches the drift before it hardens into an unspoken, unequal standard.

A closing script, for the moment right after you notice a goal you already met no longer feels like enough: "I hit the number I set. The number stopped counting because the group counting it changed, not because I failed." Say it plainly, to yourself, the moment the drift becomes visible. It won't stop the next drift from happening. It gives you, at minimum, one honest, undistorted moment of crediting yourself for something real.

When a goal gets revised upward, write down the previous version before replacing it, and keep a running file of every past target. A visible history of superseded goals makes the drift pattern impossible to miss over time, turning an invisible, ongoing process into a concrete, reviewable record you can actually hold yourself accountable to.

Set a hard ceiling, in advance, on how many times you'll let a legitimate goal be revised upward before treating the pattern itself as the thing that needs examining. One or two honest recalibrations, tied to real changes in circumstance, are reasonable. A goal that has drifted upward five or six times without ever once being met is no longer a goal — it's the drift mechanism running unchecked, and naming that plainly is often the only thing that finally interrupts it.

When setting any new financial goal, write down explicitly whether it originated from your own values or from a recent exposure to a new social context. Goals are allowed to come from both places — a new context can genuinely expand what you believe is possible, in a healthy way, not just a comparison-driven one. The point isn't to disqualify every goal touched by outside influence. It's to know, honestly, which kind of goal you're actually setting, so you can evaluate it accordingly rather than mistaking a borrowed standard for a self-chosen one.

Track exposure, not just outcomes. Once a quarter, note down which new social, professional, or neighborhood contexts you've spent meaningful time in recently. Because the drift moves through slow, cumulative exposure rather than single events, simply tracking the exposure itself gives you an early warning system for a recalibration that would otherwise only become visible well after it had already taken hold.

The rule to remember: a reference group that drifts upward every time you catch it guarantees that "enough" was never actually a destination — it was a moving target disguised as one, and the only way to catch it is to notice, every time, who moved it and why.

Chapter 3 — The Return You Didn't Chase

Why Someone Else's Lucky Trade Becomes Your Risk Tolerance

He had a plan. It was a boring plan, and he liked it that way — a broad, diversified retirement account, contributions on autopilot, a risk level chosen years ago after real thought about his age, his timeline, his tolerance for a bad year. He hadn't looked at the specific holdings in months, which was, by his own design, the entire point. A plan you don't have to watch is a plan working correctly.

Then a friend from his running group mentioned, over coffee, almost apologetically, that a single stock he'd put a modest amount into eighteen months ago had more than tripled. Not a fortune. Not retire-tomorrow money. But enough of a number, said in a casual enough tone, that it lodged itself somewhere behind his sternum and stayed there for the rest of the day. He went home and did something he hadn't done in months: he opened his own account and actually looked at it, not because anything about his plan had changed, but because something about how he felt about his plan had changed, in the span of one conversation over coffee, and he needed to see the numbers to figure out what to do about a feeling he couldn't yet name.

Within a week, he'd moved a meaningful percentage of his account into something considerably more concentrated and considerably more volatile than anything in his original plan — not a wild bet, nothing reckless enough that he'd have described it that way to himself, but a real, measurable departure from a risk level he'd chosen deliberately and held steady for years, undone by a single conversation about a friend's luck. If you'd asked him, honestly, whether new information about the market had prompted the change, he'd have said no. If you'd asked him what actually changed, he'd have struggled to answer clearly — because the honest answer, the one underneath the answer he'd give, was simply that someone else got lucky, and watching it happen made his own careful plan feel, suddenly, insufficiently ambitious.

A different version plays out over a longer stretch of years. A woman in her early forties has run a modest, low-risk small business for over a decade — profitable, stable, unglamorous, exactly the business she set out to build. A former classmate from business school took a far riskier path, raised outside investment, scaled fast, and eventually sold the company for a number substantial enough that it became, within their small alumni circle, a kind of quiet legend. The woman's business hasn't changed. Her numbers haven't gotten worse. But her sense of her own choices has shifted considerably, and it shows up specifically in how she now evaluates new opportunities — a partnership that would have felt like an unnecessary risk five years ago now feels, increasingly, like the kind of bet she "should" have been willing to make all along, measured against a single, spectacularly successful outlier from a graduating class of several hundred people whose other, far more common outcomes she's never once bothered to track.

A third scene, smaller in scale but familiar in shape: a group of coworkers who occasionally discuss their retirement accounts over lunch has, without ever formally deciding to, developed a kind of informal one-upmanship around returns — not competitive in any explicit sense, nobody keeping score out loud, but real enough that one member of the group, after hearing a colleague describe a strong quarter, quietly shifted his own contributions toward a more aggressive allocation the following week, driven by nothing more than the accumulated weight of several lunches spent hearing about other people's better numbers.

What's actually happening

The mechanism at work here runs through several interlocking layers, and it's worth taking them one at a time, because each explains a different piece of why a single data point from someone else's life can override a carefully built plan of your own.

It's worth being specific about why financial envy in particular tends to bypass the deliberate, careful thinking a person would normally apply to a major money decision. Most of the decisions covered elsewhere in a person's financial life get made slowly, with research, with comparison shopping, with genuine deliberation. Envy-driven reallocation is different in kind — it moves fast, often within days of the triggering conversation, precisely because it isn't really being processed as a financial decision at all while it's happening. It's being processed as an emotional response that happens to have financial consequences, which means it skips past most of the deliberate safeguards a person would normally apply before moving real money.

The first layer is envy, and it's worth naming plainly rather than softening, because the research on it is more specific and more useful than the word's casual meaning suggests. Psychologists Niels van de Ven and Marcel Zeelenberg, building on a substantial body of earlier research into the emotion, have documented a meaningful distinction between what they call **benign envy** and **malicious envy** — benign envy motivating a person to work harder to reach a similar outcome for themselves, malicious envy motivating a desire to see the other person's advantage diminished rather than one's own position improved. The man reallocating his portfolio after his friend's lucky stock is experiencing something close to benign envy in its purest, most financially consequential form — not wishing his friend ill, genuinely happy for him, and simultaneously moved to action in a direction that has nothing to do with sound financial planning and everything to do with narrowing a gap that opened over a single cup of coffee.

The second layer draws directly on Daniel Kahneman and Amos Tversky's prospect theory, specifically the concept of a shifting **reference point** — the baseline against which gains and losses get evaluated, which is not fixed, but moves based on context, expectation, and recent information. Before the coffee conversation, the man's reference point for what counted as a reasonable return was his own plan's steady, unremarkable, historically sound performance. After the conversation, his reference point silently updated to include his friend's tripled stock as a live possibility — which means his own perfectly good returns, unchanged in absolute terms, now registered, relative to the new reference point, as a kind of loss. This is precisely why the decision to take on more risk felt, to him, less like a gamble and more like course-correcting toward what should have been possible all along. The reference point moved. The plan didn't change. The feeling that the plan was suddenly inadequate came entirely from the gap between the two.

There's a third mechanism worth understanding in real depth, because it explains why this pattern is so specifically dangerous in the domain of investing rather than in most other financial decisions: research on **informational cascades**, developed substantially by economists Sushil Bikhchandani, David Hirshleifer, and Ivo Welch, describes how individuals, observing the choices of others, will rationally — or at least understandably — discount their own private information and follow the visible behavior of the group instead, especially under uncertainty. Investing is a domain defined by uncertainty almost by definition, which makes it an unusually fertile ground for cascades to form. A single friend's success doesn't need to be statistically meaningful to trigger a cascade response. It only needs to be visible, recent, and attached to someone who feels similar enough to be a fair comparison — all three conditions the running-group friend satisfied without either of them realizing what kind of decision was actually being set in motion over coffee.

A fourth mechanism deserves specific attention here: the **availability heuristic**, documented extensively by Kahneman and Tversky, describes how people estimate the likelihood or typicality of an outcome based on how easily examples of it come to mind, rather than on its actual statistical frequency. A single vivid story — a tripled stock, a business sold for a legendary sum — is far more available to memory than the much larger, much less memorable population of ordinary, unremarkable outcomes surrounding it: the friends who bought similarly risky positions and lost money, the classmates whose start-ups failed quietly and were never discussed at a reunion. The woman comparing her stable business against her classmate's spectacular exit is, without realizing it, comparing her own real, representative outcome against a wildly unrepresentative sample of one — the single most available story in a graduating class of several hundred, most of whose actual outcomes never became stories at all, because unremarkable outcomes rarely do.

There's a fifth mechanism worth naming, because it explains why groups — like the lunch table of coworkers — produce this effect even without any single dramatic story driving it: research on **social proof**, most thoroughly synthesized by psychologist

Robert Cialdini, describes how people use the behavior and apparent success of others as a heuristic for what constitutes correct or sensible action, particularly under uncertainty where a clear, objective standard is hard to identify. A pattern of mildly better-than-average quarters, mentioned casually and repeatedly across enough lunches, functions as a form of social proof even though no single mention would ever qualify as compelling evidence on its own — the accumulated weight of repeated, casual social signals doing the persuasive work that no individual data point could do by itself.

There's a sixth mechanism worth adding, because it explains why the reallocation, once made, so rarely gets reversed even after the initial emotional charge has faded: research on **sunk cost and commitment escalation**, extending from behavioral economics research popularized substantially by economist Richard Thaler, describes how a decision already acted on becomes psychologically harder to reverse than the same decision would have been to simply avoid making in the first place, because reversing it requires admitting the original move was a mistake rather than simply declining to make a new one.

The man who reallocated a portion of his account after his friend's tripled stock is now facing a second, quieter comparison problem layered on top of the first — reversing the reallocation means confronting, directly, that the emotional decision was the wrong one, which is a harder admission to make than simply never having made the move at all.

There's an seventh mechanism worth adding, because it explains why financial envy specifically, more than most other kinds, tends to move people toward action rather than simply toward feeling: research distinguishing **outcome envy** from **process envy** describes a meaningful difference between wanting what someone else has and wanting to have done what they did to get it. A tripled stock is an outcome that arrived largely through luck and timing, not process — the friend didn't do anything unusually skillful, and on some level the man reallocating his account knows this. But outcome envy doesn't require admiring the process to still motivate a person to chase the same category of outcome, which is part of why the reallocation happens even when, if asked directly, the man would readily admit his friend's success involved more luck than strategy.

There's a eighth piece worth naming: research on **regret aversion** in decision-making under uncertainty describes how people weigh the anticipated pain of a decision they'll regret more heavily than a comparably sized potential gain, and that this weighting shifts specifically when a comparison target is present. Before the coffee conversation, the man's plan carried no visible alternative to regret against. After it, "staying the boring course" now carries an imagined, specific counterfactual — the return he could have chased and didn't — which makes inaction itself feel, for the first time, like the riskier of the two options, even though nothing about the actual underlying probabilities of either choice has changed at all.

What it costs you

The most direct and measurable cost is a risk profile that no longer matches the person actually living with it. A plan built deliberately, around a real, considered assessment of timeline, temperament, and goals, gets quietly overridden by a reactive decision made in the emotional aftermath of someone else's news — and reactive decisions made under emotional pressure are, by a wide and consistent body of research on investor behavior, considerably more likely to be poorly timed, poorly sized, and poorly suited to the actual person making them than decisions made from a stable, considered baseline. The specific tragedy of this pattern is that it tends to strike hardest exactly when a plan was already working — the reallocation almost never happens during a genuinely bad stretch that calls for real reconsideration. It happens during an ordinary, unremarkable stretch, disrupted by someone else's extraordinary one.

There's a compounding cost tied specifically to timing. Envy-driven reallocation, by its nature, happens after the triggering event has already occurred — after the friend's stock has already tripled, after the classmate's company has already sold. Following someone else's outcome into a similar position after the fact means entering at a fundamentally different, usually far less favorable point than the person whose success triggered the reaction in the first place. This is one of the more reliable and least discussed ways ordinary people underperform their own original plans: not through bad luck in the market broadly, but through a specific, repeatable pattern of chasing yesterday's outlier at exactly the point where chasing it stops being a reasonable bet.

There's a psychological cost as well, one that outlasts any single reallocation decision. A person who has, even once, abandoned a considered plan in response to someone else's outcome tends to become more susceptible to the same pattern the next time it presents itself — each instance making the underlying reference point a little more porous, a little more willing to shift based on the next vivid story that comes along. This produces, over years, a financial life driven less by a stable, examined set of values and more by whichever compelling anecdote happened to arrive most recently, a genuinely destabilizing way to manage decisions that, by their nature, need to be evaluated over decades rather than in reaction to a single week's news.

There's a final cost worth naming, specific to how this pattern damages a person's relationship with their own original judgment. The man who built a careful plan and held it steady for years had every reason to trust that judgment. The moment he abandoned it in response to a single conversation, he didn't just change his portfolio — he taught himself, in some quiet, cumulative way, that his own careful thinking is less reliable than the next vivid story he happens to hear, which makes every future plan he builds a little more fragile, a little more provisional, a little more likely to be abandoned the next time somebody else gets lucky in front of him.

There's a cost worth naming that plays out specifically in how a household discusses money after an envy-driven decision has been made. Once a reallocation or a career risk has been taken in response to someone else's outcome, admitting the actual origin of that decision — a conversation over coffee, a story at a lunch table — becomes considerably harder than admitting to a decision made from a genuinely reasoned analysis, because the first admission requires acknowledging that a meaningful financial choice was driven by a feeling rather than a plan. This produces a specific, quiet form of financial dishonesty inside otherwise honest households: not lying about the numbers, but retroactively constructing a more rational-sounding justification for a decision that was, in its actual origin, considerably less rational than the story now being told about it, including to oneself.

There's a cost worth naming that's specific to how this pattern interacts with a person's broader relationship to their own patience. A financial plan built around a long timeline depends on trusting that patience will eventually pay off — and every envy-driven deviation, even a small one, quietly erodes that trust a little further, teaching the part of the mind responsible for sticking with a long plan that patience is negotiable the moment a sufficiently compelling story comes along. Over enough repetitions, this can produce a person who no longer really believes in their own long-term plan at all, even while continuing to nominally follow it, because some part of them has learned, through direct experience, that the plan gets abandoned whenever something more exciting shows up.

There's a cost worth naming that plays out specifically at the level of a household budget over a full market cycle. A pattern of envy-driven reallocation, repeated across several triggering conversations over several years, tends to produce a portfolio that's been assembled less like a coherent plan and more like a scrapbook of other people's best moments — a position taken here because of one friend's story, a shift made there because of a different acquaintance's news, none of it coordinated against a single, coherent view of the actual investor's own goals and risk tolerance. A portfolio built this way is often harder to evaluate honestly, because its actual, current risk level no longer matches what its owner would describe if asked to summarize their own strategy in a single sentence — the strategy on paper and the strategy actually running have quietly diverged, one comparison at a time.

The overrides

Tell one trusted person about the triggering story before making any resulting decision, and ask them, specifically, whether it sounds like sound reasoning or an emotional reaction. An outside perspective, brought in deliberately before a decision rather than after, is considerably better at spotting envy dressed up as analysis than the person actually experiencing the envy is likely to be in the moment.

Separate the emotional trigger from the financial decision by at least a week, formally, every time. When a comparison-driven urge to change your risk profile shows up, write down the trigger — the specific conversation, the specific number — and set a firm date, no sooner than a week out, before revisiting whether any change is actually warranted. Nearly all of the emotional charge behind these decisions fades measurably within days; the ones that still feel justified after the delay are worth a real, calm evaluation. The ones that don't were never about your plan to begin with.

Talk to at least one person about the full picture behind a story you've been comparing yourself against, if you can do so without prying. A single honest conversation about what actually went into a friend's success — the specific luck, the specific risks that didn't pan out along the way, the parts that never made it into the version told at dinner — very often dissolves far more of the envy than any amount of private reasoning can, because it replaces an imagined, flattened story with a real, complicated one.

Ask explicitly: what is the base rate, not just the story? For every vivid, envy-triggering success you hear about, deliberately estimate how many similar bets, made by similar people, didn't pay off — even though you'll never hear those stories at a dinner table or over coffee. You don't need an exact number. You need the reminder that the story you heard is, almost by definition, an outlier, or it wouldn't have been worth telling.

Revisit your original risk tolerance in writing, and treat any deviation from it as a decision that requires the same rigor the original plan required. If your considered risk tolerance was built through real thought about your timeline and temperament, a decision to abandon it deserves at least that much thought too — not a reaction assembled in the hours after a triggering conversation, evaluated with the same seriousness you'd have wanted applied to the original plan.

When you notice envy specifically, name it as envy rather than as new information. "I feel envious of what happened to them" is a different, more honest, and ultimately more useful sentence than "the market has shown me my plan is too conservative." The first sentence describes a feeling worth acknowledging. The second smuggles that feeling in disguised as analysis, and only one of the two should ever be allowed to move real money.

Build a standing rule for yourself, in advance, before any triggering event occurs, about how much of a portfolio you're willing to reallocate on any single impulse, and hold to it as a hard ceiling. A pre-committed limit, decided when you're calm, is considerably more reliable than a limit you try to invent in the moment, under the exact emotional conditions this chapter has spent its length describing as unreliable.

A closing script, for the moment right after hearing about someone else's financial win: "Good for them. That's their outcome, not new information about my plan." Say it plainly, even if it feels a little stiff the first several times. The stiffness fades. What it protects — a plan you built carefully, for reasons that still hold, regardless of what happened to someone else this quarter — is worth the awkwardness of practicing a sentence out loud to yourself.

Once a year, hold your actual portfolio up against the plan you originally wrote down, position by position, and ask which pieces trace back to your own reasoning and which trace back to someone else's story. This audit doesn't require reversing anything immediately. It only requires seeing clearly which parts of your current strategy were actually chosen, and which parts were inherited from a comparison you may not even remember triggering.

Keep a short, written list of the actual reasons behind your current plan, and reread it whenever a comparison-driven urge shows up. A plan's original reasoning is easy to forget in the moment a triggering story arrives, precisely because the story is vivid and the reasoning, by comparison, is quiet and abstract. Having the reasons in writing gives the quiet version a fighting chance against the vivid one.

Distinguish outcome from process explicitly, out loud, whenever a peer's financial win triggers real envy. Ask specifically what they actually did, not just what happened to them — and if the honest answer is mostly luck and timing rather than a repeatable process, say that plainly to yourself as a way of interrupting outcome envy before it recruits your own plan into chasing a result rather than a method.

The rule to remember: someone else's lucky outcome is data about their life, not about the soundness of your plan — and the single most expensive financial mistake this chapter can name is the one made in the emotional half-life of a story that was never actually yours to act on.

Chapter 4 — The Milestone Clock

Why a Number You Never Chose Became the Only One That Counts

She turns thirty in six weeks, and she has started doing arithmetic in the shower, the way she never used to. Not arithmetic about her actual goals — she knows those numbers cold, has known them for years, built a plan around them with real care. This is a different kind of arithmetic: a specific figure, lodged in her head from somewhere she couldn't precisely trace if you asked her, that a person is supposed to have saved by the time they turn thirty. She has heard some version of this number more times than she could count — from an article skimmed once, a comment made by an older coworker, a rule of thumb repeated so often across so many contexts that it stopped feeling like an opinion and started feeling like a fact of the world, the same category of fact as a boiling point or a speed limit. Her actual savings, measured against her actual goals, are on track. Measured against the number in the shower, they are not, and the second measurement is the one that's kept her up two nights this month.

The same clock runs on other ages, for other people, with the same borrowed authority. A man turning forty finds himself doing a version of the same math about what a person his age is "supposed to" have in a retirement account, a figure he's fairly sure came from a financial planning article he read years ago and has never once verified, cross-referenced against his own actual circumstances, or questioned in any serious way — it simply arrived, at some point, and installed itself as a fact rather than an estimate. He is, by any honest measure specific to his own income, expenses, and timeline, in a reasonable position. He does not feel that way, because the feeling isn't coming from his own numbers. It's coming from a milestone he adopted secondhand, from a source he can no longer even name, applied to a life it was never actually built to describe.

A third scene plays out with even less specific origin than the first two: a couple expecting their first child finds themselves anxious about a specific, round-number college savings target neither of them can trace to any actual calculation — not a figure either of them worked out based on projected tuition, their own values around debt, or their child's actual, still-unknown educational path, but a number that simply feels like the "correct" one, absorbed from years of ambient cultural noise about what responsible parents are supposed to be saving, applied to a child who is, at the time of this particular anxious conversation, not yet six months old.

What's actually happening

It's worth pausing on why a milestone number feels more authoritative than an ordinary opinion, even though, traced honestly, it usually rests on no firmer ground than one. Part of the answer is sheer repetition — the same figure encountered independently across enough unrelated contexts starts to feel corroborated, even when every one of those contexts is ultimately drawing from the same handful of original, uncredited sources. A number that seems to arrive from everywhere accumulates a kind of borrowed credibility that no single source actually earned, which is part of why so few people, on hearing a milestone figure for the third or fourth time, ever think to ask where the first version of it actually came from.

The mechanism here differs in one important way from every comparison covered so far in this book: it doesn't involve a specific, identifiable person at all. There's no friend, no sibling, no coworker whose actual life is being measured against. The comparison target is a statistical abstraction — a generalized, faceless "everyone at this age" — and that facelessness, rather than making the comparison feel weaker, tends to make it feel stronger, because an abstract, universally cited standard is much harder to argue with than any single person's specific, flawed, visibly complicated life would be.

Sociologist Robert K. Merton's reference group theory, already introduced earlier in this book, extends naturally to this pattern: a reference group doesn't need to consist of real, known individuals to function psychologically as one. A statistical or cultural abstraction — "people your age," "responsible parents," "financially healthy thirty-year-olds" — can serve exactly the same comparison function as a specific dinner-table friend group, and in some ways more powerfully, because there's no visible, flawed individual attached to it who might complicate the comparison with inconvenient details about their own actual life. An abstraction has no debt you happen to know about, no divorce quietly straining their finances, no family money nobody talks about. It's a clean, uncomplicated standard precisely because it isn't real, and uncomplicated standards are considerably harder to argue your way out of than complicated, human ones.

A second, closely related mechanism explains why milestone numbers spread and persist so effectively even when their original source is impossible to trace: research on **social norms** and normative influence, extending from foundational work by Muzafer Sherif on how groups converge on a shared standard even in the complete absence of any objective basis for it, describes how a number repeated often enough, by enough different sources, comes to function as a norm regardless of its actual validity. Sherif's original research used an ambiguous visual illusion to show that people, faced with genuine uncertainty, will converge on a shared judgment simply because others around them seem to hold it — and once that shared judgment forms, it persists across generations of a group, passed down and repeated, long after anyone can trace where it actually originated. A financial milestone repeated across enough articles, enough casual conversations, enough overheard remarks, becomes exactly this kind of self-perpetuating norm — real enough, in its social effects, to keep someone up at night, without ever having been real in the sense of resting on any solid, individually applicable calculation at all.

A third mechanism deserves attention here: the **self-discrepancy** framework introduced in Chapter 1, developed by psychologist E. Tory Higgins, becomes especially potent when the standard being measured against is an “ought” self — a version of yourself you feel obligated to become, based on external, socially transmitted expectation — rather than an “ideal” self genuinely chosen through your own reflection. A milestone number absorbed passively from ambient cultural noise functions almost entirely as an “ought”: a standard imposed from outside, felt as an obligation rather than chosen as a goal, which Higgins’s research associates specifically with anxiety and agitation, distinct from the sadness and disappointment more typically associated with falling short of a genuinely self-chosen ideal. This is part of why milestone anxiety has such a specific, restless, shower-arithmetic quality to it — it isn't ordinary disappointment about an unmet personal goal. It's a low hum of obligation to a standard that was never actually chosen, examined, or verified in the first place.

There's a fourth mechanism worth adding: the **curse of knowledge**, studied formally by economists Colin Camerer, George Loewenstein, and Martin Weber, describes a related phenomenon where information, once absorbed, becomes very difficult to fully un-know or discount, even after its original source or reliability is called into question. A milestone number, once internalized, doesn't simply evaporate the moment you learn it was never rigorously calculated for your specific circumstances. It continues exerting influence, at some barely conscious level, precisely because the mind has already treated it as established fact for long enough that unlearning it requires active, sustained effort — considerably more effort than the passive absorption that installed it in the first place ever required.

A fifth mechanism worth naming: research on **round number bias** in judgment and decision-making — the well-documented tendency for people to treat round, clean figures as inherently more meaningful, more significant thresholds than the actual underlying data would justify — helps explain why milestone numbers cluster so heavily around clean figures tied to clean ages: thirty, forty, a round savings target, a tidy multiple of income. There is no meaningful financial reason a person's life should reorganize itself around a birthday ending in zero. But round numbers feel like thresholds in a way that odd, precise, individually calculated numbers never quite do, which is part of why an entire culture converges so easily on the same handful of milestone ages and figures, repeated so often that their roundness gets mistaken for rigor.

A sixth mechanism explains why milestone figures spread so efficiently through casual conversation specifically, rather than through anything resembling a formal source: research on **memorable heuristics and rule-of-thumb transmission** within cognitive psychology describes how simple, quotable rules travel through a population far more efficiently than the nuanced, caveat-laden research they're loosely based on, because simplicity itself is what makes a claim easy to remember and easy to repeat. A milestone rule condensed to a single sentence — save this multiple of your income by this age — is, by design, more transmissible than the actual underlying research it may distantly trace back to, which typically comes wrapped in assumptions about income percentile, geographic cost of living, and retirement-age targets that get stripped away entirely somewhere in the retelling, leaving only the clean, quotable, and considerably less accurate number behind.

There's an seventh mechanism worth adding: research on **temporal landmarks**, developed substantially by behavioral scientists studying how people organize their sense of time and progress, describes how round-number ages and calendar milestones function as natural checkpoints where people pause to evaluate their broader life progress — a real and often useful psychological feature in other domains, since temporal landmarks can motivate genuine goal pursuit. But that same landmark effect, applied to an unverified financial figure rather than a self-chosen goal, converts a potentially useful checkpoint into an anxiety trigger tied to a number that was never actually validated for the specific life being evaluated at that checkpoint.

There's a eighth piece worth adding, specific to why milestone anxiety often intensifies rather than resolves once a person starts actively researching the number that's troubling them: exposure to a wider range of sources during an anxious search tends to surface more milestone claims, not fewer, and different sources rarely agree with each other, producing what researchers studying **information overload and choice anxiety** describe as a paradoxical increase in distress the more a person searches for reassurance from an ambiguous, contested category of claim. Searching for the "correct" milestone number, ironically, tends to produce a wider spread of conflicting figures than not searching at all — which is worth knowing before assuming that more research will be the thing that finally settles the anxiety down.

What it costs you

The most direct cost is anxiety attached to a number that was never actually calculated for your life — a cost paid in full regardless of whether your real, individually appropriate financial position is genuinely strong. This is, in some ways, a crueler version of comparison than the ones covered in earlier chapters, because there's no specific person to correct the record against, no friend you could ask a clarifying question and discover their situation was more complicated than it looked. The milestone simply floats there, unfalsifiable, generating real distress against a standard nobody can actually produce a citation for.

There's a compounding cost in how milestone anxiety distorts genuinely sound financial planning. A savings rate or investment strategy built carefully around your actual income, actual expenses, and actual timeline can get overridden by panic tied to an arbitrary age-based figure — leading to decisions made under real financial stress that a calmer, better-informed version of the same decision would never have produced: withdrawing from a long-term investment to "catch up" to an imaginary standard, taking on a second job at real cost to health and relationships to close a gap that was never real to begin with, making an aggressive, poorly timed change to a plan that was, before the milestone anxiety hit, working exactly as intended.

There's a cost specific to how milestone numbers interact with life stages that don't match the "typical" path the milestone assumes. Someone who changed careers later in life, took time away from paid work for caregiving, immigrated and started over financially in a new country, or simply followed a nonlinear path for entirely reasonable personal reasons gets measured against a milestone built for none of these circumstances — producing a specific, unearned shame that has nothing to do with actual financial mismanagement and everything to do with a generic, one-size-fits-all number applied to a genuinely different life.

There's a final cost worth naming plainly: milestone anxiety, left unexamined, has a way of transferring itself forward, generation to generation, the same way an unreconsidered reference group can. The couple anxious about a college savings figure for a six-month-old is, in a very real sense, pre-installing the same milestone-clock anxiety in a child who hasn't yet had a single original financial thought of their own — passing down not a specific number, necessarily, but the underlying instinct to measure a life against an untraceable, borrowed standard rather than a genuinely examined one.

There's a cost worth naming that touches specifically on how milestone anxiety shapes a person's willingness to celebrate their own genuine progress. Because the milestone functions as a pass-fail threshold rather than a continuous measure, progress that falls just short of the borrowed number tends to register, emotionally, as failure rather than as the substantial, real progress it usually actually represents — a person who has saved eighty percent of an arbitrary milestone figure often feels closer to having failed than to having accomplished something genuinely significant, purely because the threshold framing erases everything short of full completion, a framing effect that a self-built, individually calibrated goal rarely produces with the same harshness.

There's a cost worth naming that's specific to how milestone anxiety interacts with genuinely major decisions made under real time pressure — a mortgage application, a retirement date, a decision about when to start a family. Because these decisions often coincide with the same round-number ages that milestone figures cluster around, the anxiety and the decision arrive at the same moment, which means a genuinely important, carefully considered choice can end up contaminated by an unrelated, unverified milestone simply because of unfortunate timing — a thirtieth birthday landing in the same season as a home-buying decision, for instance, with the milestone anxiety quietly pushing the decision to move faster or larger than the actual numbers would otherwise support.

There's a cost worth naming that's easy to overlook because it shows up as a kind of silence rather than a visible symptom: milestone anxiety discourages people from talking honestly with each other about money, because admitting to falling short of a widely cited, seemingly authoritative number feels considerably more shameful than admitting to falling short of a private, individually calculated goal nobody else has heard of. This silence cuts people off from exactly the kind of honest peer conversation that might otherwise have revealed the milestone was never well-founded to begin with — the shame the milestone produces actively prevents the correction that would relieve it, a closed loop that can run for years without anyone involved saying a word about it out loud.

The overrides

When you feel the specific dread of an approaching round-number birthday, write down what's actually changing about your life versus what's simply a date on a calendar. Separating the real, substantive changes from the purely symbolic ones strips a milestone birthday of much of its borrowed authority, leaving only the parts of the anxiety that are actually tied to something real.

Trace the number back to its actual source before treating it as fact. For any milestone figure currently generating real anxiety, spend ten minutes trying to find where it actually came from — a specific study, a specific article, a specific calculation, with its assumptions stated plainly. Most milestone numbers, traced back far enough, turn out to rest on assumptions — about income level, cost of living, family structure — that have nothing to do with your actual circumstances, and seeing the mismatch in black and white does more to dissolve the anxiety than any amount of reassurance ever could.

Build your own milestone from your own numbers, in writing, and treat it as the only legitimate one. A savings target calculated from your actual income, actual expenses, and actual timeline is not just more accurate than a borrowed cultural figure — it's the only kind of milestone capable of actually being met, since it was built to describe your life rather than a generic, statistical one.

When milestone anxiety strikes, ask whether it's an "ought" or an "ideal." If the number feels like an obligation imposed from outside rather than a goal you'd have chosen on your own reflection, name it as an "ought" explicitly. Obligations borrowed from ambient cultural noise carry far less real authority than they feel like they do in the moment, and naming the feeling correctly is often enough to loosen its grip.

Actively seek out the range, not the single number, whenever a milestone claim surfaces. Any honest accounting of financial outcomes at a given age is a wide range, not a single figure — and deliberately reminding yourself of the range, rather than the falsely precise midpoint that tends to circulate, is usually enough to defuse the specific panic a round number produces.

For milestones tied to a child's future, delay setting any target until there's enough real information to calculate one honestly. A savings goal for a six-month-old, built from actual, current data about cost trajectories and your own actual capacity, revisited periodically as circumstances become clearer, will always be a sounder foundation than a number absorbed from ambient anxiety before there was anything real yet to calculate against.

A closing script, for the moment a milestone number surfaces uninvited: "That's a number about a life I'm not living. My number is the one I actually calculated." Practice it enough times that it becomes the automatic first response to the next borrowed figure that tries to install itself as fact — because the next one will arrive, and the automatic response is what actually stops it from taking hold the way the last one did.

Say the real number out loud to at least one other person, even if it doesn't match the milestone. Breaking the silence this pattern depends on — telling a trusted friend or partner your actual savings figure, and how it compares to a milestone you've been quietly measuring against — very often reveals that the milestone was carrying far less authority than the private anxiety around it ever suggested.

Treat any milestone number attached to a specific age as a hypothesis to test against your own life, never a verdict to accept on arrival. A hypothesis gets checked against evidence and revised or discarded accordingly. A verdict gets absorbed and carried. Holding a milestone figure as the former rather than the latter changes its entire relationship to your sense of self-worth, even before you've finished checking whether it actually applies to you.

Separate the temporal landmark from the milestone figure explicitly. Use a round-number birthday or a new year as a genuine checkpoint for reviewing your own self-chosen goals, deliberately stripped of any borrowed comparison figure — the landmark itself is a useful prompt for reflection; the unverified number riding along with it is not.

The rule to remember: a milestone you can't trace to an actual calculation isn't a standard — it's a rumor that got repeated often enough to sound like arithmetic, and the only

number worth losing sleep over is the one you built yourself.

Chapter 5 — The Sibling Standard

Why the Scoreboard Never Actually Left the Family Table

Thanksgiving has a rhythm now, and everyone at the table knows it without ever discussing it out loud. Somewhere between the meal and the dishes, in the loose, unstructured hour where conversation drifts, the topic will turn — never announced as such, always arriving sideways, through a mention of a home renovation, a new car in the driveway, a comment about a job that's "going really well" — toward the two brothers' relative standing, a comparison every single person at the table can feel operating even though nobody would ever call it that if you asked them directly. The older brother built a stable, unremarkable career in a field their father respects deeply. The younger brother took a riskier, less conventional path that's recently started paying off in a way that's become impossible not to notice. Their mother doesn't keep score, she'd tell you, genuinely believing it. And yet she has, without fail, for three years running, found some way to work each brother's recent milestone into a conversation with the other one, framed as innocent sharing of family news, landing, every single time, as something closer to a scorecard read aloud.

Neither brother would describe their relationship as competitive. They talk on the phone regularly, genuinely enjoy each other's company, would show up for each other without hesitation in any real crisis. And still, each of them can recite the other's approximate financial trajectory with a precision neither applies to any other person in their life, tracking a comparison that started, as far as either of them could tell you, sometime around adolescence and has simply never fully stopped running since — updated at every holiday, every family group text, every unplanned mention from a parent who insists, sincerely, that she's not comparing them at all.

The same pattern surfaces with sharper edges once a parent's estate becomes part of the picture. Three adult siblings, each doing reasonably well in entirely different ways — one a business owner, one in a stable salaried career, one having chosen a lower-paying but personally meaningful path in a helping profession — find themselves, in the months after their father's death, locked in a set of tensions around his estate that have almost nothing to do with the actual dollar amounts involved and almost everything to do with a decades-old sibling scoreboard finally getting a chance to render a kind of final verdict. The business owner feels, unspoken but real, that his greater financial success should be irrelevant to an equal split, a matter of principle. The sibling in the helping profession feels, equally unspoken, that a slightly larger share would only be fair given the income gap the other two have enjoyed for years. Nobody says any of this directly. The disagreement gets litigated instead through arguments about specific possessions, specific line items, specific procedural questions about the will — proxy fights standing in for a scoreboard that's been running since childhood and has never once been openly discussed by any of the three people whose entire adult relationship it's been quietly shaping.

A third scene plays out with lower stakes but the same underlying architecture: two sisters, close in age, close in relationship, find that every visit home reliably produces a specific tension neither of them enjoys and neither of them can quite name — a comparison of houses, of husbands' careers, of which sister's children are enrolled in which kind of school, run continuously by their extended family, by old family friends who ask pointed, comparative questions at every gathering, and, increasingly, by the sisters themselves, against each other, in a habit neither of them remembers consciously choosing to develop.

What's actually happening

It's worth naming, before going further, why the family scoreboard so rarely gets discussed directly even in families that are otherwise close and communicative. Most families have real, working norms against openly ranking their own members — it violates an implicit rule about unconditional love, the idea that a parent's or a sibling's regard shouldn't be contingent on comparative success. This norm is genuinely valuable in most respects. It also means the comparison, when it happens, has to happen indirectly, disguised as ordinary news-sharing, precisely because the family's own values forbid the direct version — which paradoxically makes the indirect version harder to catch and address, since naming it plainly can feel, itself, like a violation of the same unconditional-love norm the family is trying to protect.

Family comparison operates through a set of mechanisms distinct from the general social comparison covered in earlier chapters, and it's worth understanding why the family version tends to run deeper, longer, and with more emotional force than comparison against a friend, coworker, or stranger ever quite manages to.

The first and most foundational mechanism comes from **social comparison theory** itself, but specifically from research extending Festinger's original framework into questions of *who* people compare themselves against most intensely. The research consistently finds that comparison is strongest, most automatic, and most emotionally charged against people perceived as similar on dimensions that matter — and few comparisons offer more perceived similarity than a sibling, who shares genetics, upbringing, household resources, and, very often, near-identical starting conditions in a way almost no other comparison target in a person's life can match. A stranger's success can be dismissed as the product of different circumstances. A sibling's success, having emerged from what looks, at least on the surface, like the exact same starting conditions, resists that dismissal far more effectively — which is precisely why sibling comparison tends to carry a sharper, more personal sting than comparison against almost anyone else.

A second, related mechanism comes from research on **birth order and family systems**, drawing on the broader tradition of family systems theory developed substantially by psychiatrist Murray Bowen, describes how children within the same family are frequently assigned, consciously or not, distinct roles by parents and the family system as a whole — the responsible one, the ambitious one, the creative one, the one who needs looking after — roles that tend to calcify early and persist, often unexamined, well into adulthood, shaping not just how family members see each other but how each sibling comes to see and evaluate themselves. A sibling assigned the "responsible" role early in life may find themselves, decades later, still measuring their own financial choices against an internalized expectation installed by that role, regardless of whether it still fits the adult they've actually become.

A third mechanism deserves careful attention, because it explains why parents so often insist, sincerely, that they aren't comparing their children while doing exactly that: research on **differential parental treatment**, a well-established area within developmental psychology, has documented that parents, even parents who consciously value and intend to practice equal treatment, very often do treat children differently in measurable, real ways — attention, praise, financial support, expressed pride — and that children, across a large and consistent body of studies, register these differences with far greater sensitivity and accuracy than parents themselves typically believe they do. The mother at Thanksgiving who insists she doesn't keep score is very likely being honest about her own conscious intention. She is also, per this research, very likely wrong about the actual, observable effect of her behavior — because differential treatment doesn't require conscious intent to register clearly with the children on its receiving end, then or decades later.

A fourth mechanism is specific to why estate and inheritance situations activate this pattern so intensely: research on **equity theory** within social psychology, developed substantially by psychologist J. Stacy Adams, describes how people evaluate fairness not by absolute outcomes but by a ratio of inputs to outcomes, compared against a relevant reference — and few reference points feel more relevant, more inescapably comparable, than a sibling whose entire life has served as an ongoing, lifelong comparison point. An estate split that would strike an outside observer as perfectly fair — an equal division among adult children — can feel, to siblings each carrying a lifetime of accumulated comparison, like a verdict on decades of relative worth rather than a simple, neutral administrative outcome, because the money, by the time it actually arrives, was never really just money. It arrived carrying the entire scoreboard with it.

A fifth mechanism worth naming: psychologists studying **social comparison within close relationships** specifically — as distinct from comparison against strangers or distant acquaintances — have found that comparison against someone you're also emotionally close to produces a specific, complicated blend of genuine happiness for the other person's success and genuine discomfort about your own relative position, experienced simultaneously rather than as a simple, single emotion. This dual, contradictory experience is part of why sibling comparison so rarely gets named honestly even by the people living inside it — admitting to discomfort about a sibling's success can feel, wrongly but powerfully, like evidence of not loving them enough, when in fact both feelings are simply true at once, and neither one cancels the other out.

There's a sixth mechanism worth naming, and it's specific to why the scoreboard tends to sharpen rather than soften with age, contrary to what most families would predict about themselves: research on **life-course comparison** within family sociology has found that as siblings move further from a shared childhood and further into distinct, harder-to-compare adult lives — different cities, different careers, different family structures — the comparison doesn't fade for lack of common ground. It often intensifies, because the increasingly divergent paths make each sibling's specific choices feel more like evidence for a genuine, resolvable question of who chose correctly, rather than simply two different people living two different, equally valid lives.

There's an seventh mechanism worth adding, and it explains why sibling comparison tends to feel especially loaded around money specifically, more than around most other life domains siblings might otherwise compare: money is unusually well-suited to functioning as a proxy for a much older, harder-to-name childhood question — which of us was loved more, valued more, believed in more. Financial success, in this light, isn't just being measured for its own sake. It's being read, often unconsciously, as evidence in a much older case about parental regard, which is part of why a sibling's financial update can trigger a response wildly disproportionate to the actual dollar amount involved — the dollar amount was never really the whole question being asked.

There's a eighth piece worth naming: research on **triangulation** within family systems theory describes how a third party — often a parent, but sometimes another relative — can unintentionally sustain a comparison dynamic between two people by relaying information between them that neither would otherwise have sought out directly. The mother at Thanksgiving isn't just failing to notice her own comparisons. She's functioning, structurally, as an information conduit neither brother asked for, ensuring each stays continuously updated on the other's milestones through a channel that feels, to her, like ordinary family news-sharing, but that operates, in practice, as the exact mechanism keeping the scoreboard running at full speed between two adults who might otherwise have let their own direct contact naturally slow the comparison down.

What it costs you

The most direct cost is a financial decision-making process contaminated by a scoreboard that has nothing to do with your own actual goals, values, or circumstances, running since a period of life — often childhood or adolescence — during which none of the people involved had any real say in how the comparison got established. A person who takes on excessive risk, or pushes for a career path that doesn't genuinely suit them, or makes a major financial decision specifically to "catch up" to a sibling's trajectory, is making that decision in service of a scoreboard installed decades earlier by forces entirely outside their control — a family dynamic, a differential-treatment pattern, a role assigned before either sibling was old enough to consent to it.

There's a compounding cost specific to how sibling comparison distorts genuinely important family decisions — estate planning, decisions about caring for aging parents, questions about shared family property — turning what should be practical, collaborative decisions into proxy battles for a much older, much less resolvable question about relative worth. This is, in many families, the single most corrosive cost of the pattern: it takes decisions that could otherwise be handled with straightforward practicality and infuses them with decades of accumulated emotional weight that has almost nothing to do with the decision actually on the table.

There's a relational cost that compounds over an entire lifetime rather than a single decision. Siblings who spend decades quietly comparing financial trajectories, even while maintaining warm, functional relationships on the surface, often carry an undercurrent of guardedness into money-related family conversations that never fully resolves — a caution around discussing real numbers, a reluctance to ask for help even when help would be reasonable, a performance of not-quite-full honesty about one's own financial situation specifically with the one or two people in the world who share the most context for understanding it. The scoreboard doesn't just distort decisions. It quietly limits how much genuine, honest support siblings are willing to offer or accept from each other, at precisely the moments in life — a job loss, a health crisis, a difficult stretch — when that support would matter most.

There's a final cost worth naming, and it belongs to the next generation as much as the current one: children who grow up watching a sibling scoreboard run at every family gathering absorb the pattern as a working model of how family and money relate to each other, often before they're old enough to consciously evaluate whether it's a model worth keeping. The scoreboard, left unexamined, doesn't stay contained to one generation. It tends to install itself in the next one too, passed down not through any deliberate teaching, but simply through repeated exposure to what "normal" looks like at a family table.

There's a cost worth naming that touches specifically on how a sibling scoreboard affects each sibling's willingness to be genuinely vulnerable about a real financial setback. A person who has spent years positioned, in the family's unspoken accounting, as "the successful one" often finds it considerably harder to admit to a real financial struggle when one eventually arrives, precisely because doing so threatens a family role that's become part of their identity, not just their bank balance. This can lead to genuinely dangerous silence during exactly the moments a family's support would matter most — a business failing quietly, a debt spiraling unaddressed — because admitting the trouble would require dismantling a scoreboard position that took decades to build.

There's a cost worth naming that runs through how adult siblings handle joint financial responsibility for aging parents specifically. A family scoreboard that's been running for decades rarely stays contained once a parent begins to need real, practical financial support — contributions toward care, decisions about a parent's home, shared responsibility for medical costs. Siblings carrying an unexamined comparison history often find these genuinely practical conversations distorted by decades-old questions about fairness and relative standing that have nothing to do with the actual, present-tense logistics of caring for a parent, making an already difficult family transition considerably harder than the practical facts alone would require.

There's a cost worth naming that shows up specifically in how the scoreboard shapes which sibling gets asked for help, and which sibling offers it, during a genuine family crisis. A family running an unexamined financial comparison for decades often develops an unspoken, calcified assumption about which sibling is "the successful one" and which is "the one who struggles" — an assumption that can persist well past the point where it's still accurate, leading a family to overlook a genuinely capable sibling's ability to help during a crisis, or to place an unfair, ongoing burden on the sibling assumed to be doing best, regardless of whether that sibling's actual current circumstances still support the role the scoreboard assigned them years earlier.

The overrides

Ask yourself, honestly, which family role you were assigned before you turned ten, and whether any of your

current financial decisions are still quietly performing it. The responsible one still overworking to justify a label given by a third-grade teacher's praise, the struggling one still underselling real strengths because struggling became a familiar, almost comfortable identity — naming the original role, out loud, is often the fastest way to loosen its grip on decisions being made decades later, by an adult who never actually agreed to keep playing the part.

Name the scoreboard directly, once, in a low-stakes moment — not during a conflict, not around an estate decision, but in an ordinary conversation. Something as simple as "I've noticed we sometimes compare our finances without really meaning to — I don't want that between us" can do more to defuse a decades-old dynamic than years of quietly enduring it ever will, precisely because the scoreboard depends on staying unnamed to keep operating unchallenged.

Separate practical family decisions from the scoreboard explicitly, in writing, before they need to be made. Estate plans, caregiving arrangements, and shared property decisions made calmly, in advance, and grounded in explicit, agreed-upon principles are far less likely to become proxy battlegrounds than decisions made reactively, under emotional pressure, after a parent's death or health crisis has already activated every old family dynamic at once.

When you notice yourself tracking a sibling's financial trajectory with more precision than you'd apply to anyone else, ask what role you were assigned early on, and whether you're still unconsciously performing it. The "responsible one," the "ambitious one," the "one who needs help" — these roles rarely get consciously chosen, and rarely get consciously retired either, unless someone deliberately notices they're still running and decides, on purpose, whether they still fit.

Practice being honestly, specifically happy for a sibling's success without immediately running your own comparison against it. This is harder than it sounds, and it's fine if it doesn't come naturally at first — the goal isn't to eliminate the discomfort instantly, but to notice it, let it exist without acting on it, and respond to the sibling in front of you rather than to the scoreboard running in the background.

If a parent insists they don't compare their children, believe their intention and gently, separately, ask about the effect anyway. "I know you don't mean to compare us, and I want to mention that it sometimes lands that way" respects the parent's sincerity while still naming the real, documented gap between intention and effect that this pattern's research consistently finds.

A closing script, for the moment a comparison surfaces at a family gathering: "That's their path. I'm glad it's working for them, and it doesn't change how I feel about mine." Say it internally if saying it out loud doesn't fit the moment. The sentence doesn't need an audience to do its work — it needs to interrupt the scoreboard calculation before it fully runs, which it can do whether or not anyone else at the table ever hears it.

If a parent or relative habitually relays comparative news between siblings, ask them directly to stop, kindly and specifically. "I'd rather hear updates about my brother from him directly, when he wants to share them" names the triangulation without requiring an accusation, and often does more to slow a family scoreboard than any amount of private effort by the siblings themselves.

When you catch yourself reading a sibling's update as evidence in an old case about parental regard, name that specifically rather than letting it stay disguised as a financial reaction. "This isn't really about the house — it's about whether I felt as valued growing up" is a harder sentence to say than a comment about real estate, and it's also the sentence that actually addresses what's driving the reaction.

Before a shared responsibility for an aging parent arrives, discuss it explicitly, separate from any conversation about relative sibling success. Agreeing in advance on principles — proportional to income, split evenly regardless of income, or another explicit standard — while the topic is still hypothetical removes most of the room for a decades-old scoreboard to hijack a conversation that should be about a parent's actual needs.

The rule to remember: a sibling scoreboard installed in childhood doesn't expire on its own — it keeps running,

quietly, at every holiday and every family decision, until someone in the family finally says its name out loud.

Chapter 6 — The Downward Comparison Trap

Why Feeling Better Than Someone Else Isn't the Same as Doing Well

It's a specific kind of relief, and she feels it every time her cousin calls to vent about money — a real, physical loosening in her chest, the same relief you'd feel putting down something heavy you didn't realize you'd been carrying. Her cousin's finances are, by any honest measure, in real trouble: mounting credit card debt, an underwater car loan, a pattern of decisions that would worry anyone who cared about her. And every call, every fresh detail of the latest financial setback, produces in this woman a quiet, unmistakable sense that her own situation, whatever its actual shortcomings, is fine — genuinely fine, nothing to worry about, evidenced not by her own numbers but by how much better those numbers look next to her cousin's.

The trouble is that her own numbers, examined honestly and on their own terms, aren't actually fine. She's been carrying a persistent, low-grade credit card balance for three years that never seems to shrink no matter how many months she tells herself this is the month she'll pay it down. Her retirement contributions lapsed eighteen months ago when a stretch of unexpected expenses hit, and she's never quite restarted them. None of this feels urgent to her, has never once felt urgent to her, because urgency requires a comparison point sharp enough to trigger it, and her comparison point — her cousin, whose situation is genuinely worse — makes her own real, ongoing problems disappear into a kind of comfortable middle distance. She isn't lying to herself, exactly. She's measuring accurately. She's just measuring against the wrong thing.

The same relief shows up in a very different life. A man in his early sixties, watching a close friend's retirement plans collapse after a late-life divorce split what modest savings the friend had built, feels, uncomfortably but honestly, a version of the same downward relief — grateful his own marriage is stable, grateful his own retirement account is intact, and, underneath the genuine sympathy he feels for his friend, quietly reassured that his own retirement planning, which he hasn't seriously reviewed in nearly a decade, must be roughly on track, since it so clearly compares favorably to his friend's genuinely difficult situation. His own plan hasn't been stress-tested against anything real. It's simply been measured, repeatedly, against a friend's worse outcome, and found — by that single, badly chosen standard — adequate.

A third scene plays out at a smaller scale but the same shape: a young couple, working through real but manageable financial stress in their first years of marriage, spends an unusual amount of time discussing and, in a quiet way, savoring stories about other couples they know who are doing worse — a couple who filed for bankruptcy, a couple whose spending habits everyone privately worries about. These conversations aren't malicious; they come from a genuine place of processing anxiety. But they function, consistently, as a substitute for the harder, more useful conversation this couple has been avoiding: an honest, detailed look at their own actual budget, which downward comparison keeps making feel unnecessary.

What's actually happening

The mechanism here has real, substantial research behind it, and it's worth understanding both why downward comparison feels so genuinely good and why that good feeling is, specifically, part of the problem rather than evidence against it.

Social psychologist Thomas Ashby Wills's foundational **downward comparison theory**, developed in the early 1980s, describes a well-documented pattern in which people under threat or experiencing low self-esteem seek out comparisons with others who are worse off, specifically in order to feel better about their own situation — a genuine, measurable boost to subjective well-being that requires no actual improvement in the underlying circumstances at all. This is not a character flaw or a sign of unusual pettiness. Wills's research found this pattern to be common, adaptive in certain limited circumstances, and deeply human — a real, functioning mechanism for managing distress in the short term. The problem this chapter addresses isn't that downward comparison exists. It's that the relief it produces is so genuinely effective at reducing distress that it can substitute entirely for the harder, more useful work of actually addressing whatever's producing the distress in the first place.

A closely related second mechanism draws on research into **self-affirmation theory**, developed substantially by psychologist Claude Steele, describes how affirming one's own worth or adequacy in one domain — even a domain unrelated to the actual problem at hand — can reduce a person's motivation to engage with threatening information in the domain where the real problem lives. A downward comparison functions as exactly this kind of affirmation: it doesn't solve the credit card balance or the neglected retirement contributions, but it provides enough of a felt sense of relative adequacy that the motivation to actually confront those specific, real problems quietly diminishes, sometimes for years at a stretch.

A third mechanism deserves careful attention: research on **motivated reasoning**, a well-documented finding across social psychology and behavioral economics describing how people process information in ways that serve a desired conclusion rather than an accurate one, helps explain why downward comparisons get selected and remembered so much more readily than upward or even lateral ones, once a person has an emotional stake in feeling reassured rather than alarmed. The woman in this chapter's opening scene isn't consciously seeking out her cousin's financial struggles to feel better. But once the comparison is available, motivated reasoning ensures it gets weighted, remembered, and returned to far more readily than a more accurate, harder comparison — say, against her own stated financial goals — ever would be, because the cousin's situation delivers the conclusion she's motivated, without realizing it, to reach.

A fourth mechanism explains why downward comparison is particularly seductive in the financial domain specifically: unlike many other life domains, financial hardship is, culturally, one of the more visible and more frequently discussed forms of struggle — friends and family members do talk, sometimes at length, about debt, job loss, and financial setbacks, in a way they might not discuss other private struggles as openly. This relatively high visibility of others' financial difficulty means downward financial comparisons are simply more available, more frequently supplied by ordinary social life, than downward comparisons in most other domains — creating unusually frequent opportunities for exactly the relief-without-resolution pattern this chapter describes.

A fifth mechanism worth naming: psychologists studying **relative standing and threat regulation** describe how comparison serves not just an information function but a genuine emotion-regulation function — a way of managing anxiety about one's own situation by recruiting a comparison that produces calm rather than one that produces accurate information. This distinction matters enormously here, because it means downward comparison isn't primarily a thinking error. It's an emotional strategy, deployed, usually unconsciously, specifically because it works at calming a feeling — which is exactly why it's so much harder to simply reason your way out of than a straightforward factual mistake would be.

A sixth mechanism explains why downward comparison so often feels indistinguishable from genuine gratitude, and why that resemblance makes it especially hard to catch: research distinguishing **gratitude** from **relative relief** describes gratitude as an appreciation for what one actually has, evaluated largely on its own terms, while relative relief depends entirely on the existence of someone doing worse to measure against. The two feel remarkably similar from the inside — a warm, settled sense that things are fine — but they behave very differently under pressure. Genuine gratitude tends to hold steady even when a comparison point disappears. Relative relief evaporates the moment the worse-off comparison is no longer available, which is a useful, practical test for telling the two apart: does the calm survive when the other person's story isn't in the room anymore?

There's an seventh mechanism worth adding, because it explains why downward comparison feels so specifically kind, even virtuous, from the inside, which makes it harder to question than most other patterns in this book: expressing sympathy for someone doing worse is a genuinely prosocial act, and the warmth involved is real. The distortion this chapter describes isn't in the sympathy itself — it's in the way that sympathy gets quietly repurposed, without either party intending it, into private evidence about the sympathizer's own adequacy. A person can be simultaneously a good, caring friend to someone going through real hardship and be using that same hardship, underneath the caring, as an unexamined reassurance about their own unrelated financial problems. Both things are true at once, and only one of them is visible from the outside.

There's a eighth piece worth naming: research on **defensive avoidance** in health and financial decision-making describes a broader pattern in which people manage anxiety about a threatening topic by avoiding direct engagement with it altogether, substituting a less threatening, adjacent activity that produces some of the same relief without requiring confrontation with the actual problem. Discussing a struggling relative's finances at length functions, for many people, as exactly this kind of substitute activity — it feels like engaging seriously with money, occupies real time and real emotional energy, and produces genuine relief, all while systematically avoiding the one conversation — an honest look at your own specific numbers — that would actually move anything forward.

What it costs you

The most direct cost is delay — real, measurable delay in addressing financial problems that, left unaddressed, tend to compound rather than resolve on their own. The woman with the lingering credit card balance and the lapsed retirement contributions has, by relying on downward comparison for genuine emotional relief for three years, allowed two real, actionable problems to continue unaddressed for three years longer than they would have if her sense of urgency had been calibrated against her own goals rather than her cousin's worse situation. Interest compounds. Missed retirement contributions don't get retroactively made up. The relief was real. The cost of that relief, measured in actual dollars and actual years of lost compounding, is also real, and considerably larger than the relief itself.

There's a compounding cost specific to how downward comparison interacts with genuine financial risk. A person reassured by a worse comparison point tends to under-monitor their own actual situation — checking balances less often, reviewing plans less frequently, catching problems later than they otherwise would. This isn't laziness. It's a direct, logical consequence of feeling reassured: vigilance requires a felt sense that something might be wrong, and downward comparison is specifically effective at removing that felt sense, whether or not the underlying reality has actually improved.

There's a relational cost worth naming as well, one that's easy to overlook because it doesn't look like a cost from the inside. A pattern of finding relief in other people's financial struggles, even when never expressed unkindly, can subtly shape how a person relates to friends and family going through real hardship — treating their struggles, even with genuine sympathy intact, partly as data points in an ongoing private comparison rather than purely as difficulties deserving uncomplicated support. This rarely rises to the level of anything the struggling friend would notice or the comparing person would consciously endorse if named directly. But it's there, running quietly, and it's worth being honest about, because genuine support and comparison-driven relief are not quite the same posture toward another person's pain, even when they look identical from the outside.

There's a final cost worth naming, and it may be the most consequential of all: downward comparison substitutes a genuinely false sense of security for the real work of building one. Financial security built by comparing favorably against people doing worse is not, in any meaningful sense, actual financial security — it's a feeling, produced by a comparison, entirely disconnected from whether your own plan would actually hold up under real pressure, a real emergency, a real stretch of bad luck. The man reassured about his retirement by his friend's divorce-driven collapse has learned nothing whatsoever about whether his own decade-unreviewed plan would survive a comparable shock. He's simply stopped worrying about the question, which is a very different, and considerably more dangerous, outcome.

There's a cost worth naming that touches specifically on how downward comparison distorts a person's sense of their own agency over time. Relief that comes from someone else's worse circumstances requires nothing of the person feeling it — no plan, no change, no effort — which means it can quietly teach a person that feeling better about money doesn't actually require doing anything differently. This is a genuinely corrosive lesson, repeated often enough, because it decouples the felt sense of financial okay-ness from the actual behaviors that would produce a durable version of it, leaving a person fluent in feeling reassured and considerably less practiced at the harder, slower work of earning that reassurance honestly.

There's a cost worth naming that shows up specifically in how downward comparison affects a person's willingness to seek real, professional financial help when it's actually warranted. Someone who has spent years feeling reassured by comparison against a worse-off relative or friend often doesn't recognize their own situation as serious enough to warrant real attention — a credit counselor, a financial planner, a frank conversation with a partner about a genuinely troubling pattern — because "serious enough" has been calibrated against a much harder situation rather than against their own actual numbers. This is one of the more consequential costs in this chapter, because it doesn't just delay a decision. It can delay the specific kind of outside help that might have interrupted a genuinely worsening pattern years earlier than it eventually gets addressed.

There's a cost worth naming that's specific to couples who lean on this pattern together, as the young couple in this chapter's third scene do. Two people who habitually reassure each other through downward comparison, rather than through honest engagement with their own budget, can develop a shared, mutually reinforcing blind spot — each partner's relief validating the other's, making the pattern considerably harder for either of them to break alone than it would be for a single person doing the same thing in private. A couple's downward-comparison habit isn't just an individual coping strategy multiplied by two. It becomes, over time, a genuine shared agreement about which conversations the household is and isn't willing to have, however unspoken that agreement remains.

The overrides

Ask, plainly, what a genuinely stable financial life would actually require, independent of anyone else's situation, and compare your own numbers only against that answer. Building this independent standard once, in writing, gives you something more durable to measure against than either a discouraging upward comparison or a falsely reassuring downward one — a fixed point that doesn't move depending on who happens to be struggling or thriving nearby this month.

Separate the emotional relief from the informational content of every comparison, explicitly. When you notice a downward comparison producing genuine relief, name that relief for what it is — a real, valid feeling — and then ask, separately, whether anything about your own actual numbers has changed. Usually the honest answer is no, and naming that gap directly is often enough to keep the relief from quietly substituting for real action.

Schedule a regular, calendar-based review of your own numbers, entirely independent of any comparison, upward or downward. A quarterly check-in against your own stated goals, done as a standing habit rather than triggered by any external event, is the most reliable defense against a downward comparison quietly delaying real action — because it doesn't depend on feeling alarmed enough to act. It happens on schedule, regardless of how reassured a recent comparison happened to leave you feeling.

When a downward comparison arrives, hold the other person's difficulty and your own unresolved problem as two separate, unrelated facts, out loud if needed. "I'm genuinely sorry that's happening to them, and separately, my own credit card balance still needs attention" keeps the two facts from quietly canceling each other out the way they tend to when left unexamined.

When you catch yourself bringing up someone else's harder situation unprompted, pause and ask what you were actually hoping to feel by mentioning it. Most of the time the honest answer is relief, not concern for the other person, and simply noticing that gap between the stated and actual motive is often enough to redirect the conversation, and the private feeling underneath it, toward something more useful.

Notice which comparisons you seek out, and ask honestly whether you're gathering information or managing a feeling. If you find yourself specifically drawn to conversations or stories about people doing worse than you, during a period when your own finances have real, known problems, that pattern is worth naming directly — not as a moral failing, but as useful information about what your own comparison instinct is actually trying to accomplish for you.

Build a real stress test for your own plan, independent of anyone else's situation. Instead of relying on a friend's or relative's worse outcome to reassure you that your own plan would hold up under pressure, actually model a real disruption — a job loss, a health crisis, a divorce — against your own specific numbers. The reassurance this produces, when it's genuinely earned, is durable in a way that borrowed reassurance from someone else's hardship never quite manages to be.

A closing script, for the moment a downward comparison starts producing relief: "I'm relieved, and that relief isn't the same as evidence that I'm fine." Say it plainly to yourself, and let it sit there uncomfortably for a moment rather than resolving it immediately. The discomfort is doing useful work — it's the exact gap this chapter has spent its length describing, held open just long enough to actually look at it.

For couples, name the shared pattern out loud together, once, outside the heat of any specific conversation about a struggling friend or relative. "I think we sometimes use other people's harder situations to avoid looking closely at our own" is a sentence that can only be said calmly, in advance, and it tends to do far more work said that way than raised defensively in the middle of the next comparison-driven conversation.

Practice sitting with a struggling friend's or relative's story without immediately, even silently, running a comparison against your own situation. This is a genuine skill, not an instant switch — try simply listening, holding their difficulty as entirely their own for the length of the conversation, and notice how much harder that is than it sounds. The difficulty itself is useful information about how automatic the comparison habit has become.

Set an explicit, low threshold for seeking outside financial help, defined by your own numbers rather than by comparison to anyone else's situation. Deciding in advance — a specific balance, a specific number of months of stalled progress — that you'll consult a professional removes the decision from a threshold that downward comparison has every incentive to keep raising indefinitely.

The rule to remember: feeling better than someone else is a real feeling, and it is not the same thing as being okay —

and the two get confused most easily in exactly the moments when confusing them costs the most.

Chapter 7 — The Professional Peer Trap

Why Your Paycheck Feels Wrong the Moment You Learn Someone Else's

He liked his job on Tuesday. On Wednesday, over drinks after a work event, a colleague at a similar level, similar tenure, similar title at a different company mentioned, without any particular agenda, a number that landed somewhere north of what he made — not dramatically more, not the kind of gap that would suggest anything was seriously wrong with his own compensation, but enough of a gap, delivered casually enough, that something in him shifted for good. He went into the office on Thursday and noticed, for the first time in months, small irritations about his job he'd have shrugged off the week before. The commute felt longer. A minor disagreement with his manager felt more significant than it would have three days earlier. Nothing about his actual job had changed between Tuesday and Thursday. Only the number in his head had changed, and the number, it turned out, was doing more work in how he felt about his career than the career itself was.

The same pattern runs, often more corrosively, inside a single workplace. A woman discovers, through an accidental slip during a project planning conversation, that a colleague hired around the same time, doing work she genuinely considers comparable to her own, earns meaningfully more than she does. She spends the following weeks in a state of low-grade preoccupation she can't quite shake — reviewing her own contributions obsessively, replaying old performance conversations for clues she might have missed, feeling a specific, hard-to-name resentment not really at the colleague, who did nothing wrong, but at a system that let this gap exist for however long it's existed without her knowing. She eventually asks for a raise, and gets a partial one, and finds that even the raise doesn't fully resolve the feeling — because the feeling was never really about the absolute number. It was about the gap, and gaps, once discovered, have a way of persisting in memory long after the specific dollar difference that produced them has narrowed.

A third scene involves no direct disclosure at all, just an inference built from indirect evidence. A freelance graphic designer, comparing his own rates against a rough, informal sense of what peers in his specific niche seem to be charging — gathered from scattered, half-remembered comments in a professional community, from the occasional posted rate card, from nothing especially rigorous or reliable — has spent two years feeling persistently underpriced, adjusting his own rates upward periodically not based on his actual demand, his actual expertise, or his actual cost of doing business, but based on a shifting, imprecise sense of where "everyone else" seems to be pricing themselves, gathered from a sample size and reliability he's never once seriously interrogated.

What's actually happening

It's worth being specific about why professional compensation, out of every category of information a peer might disclose, carries such disproportionate weight. A house, a vacation, a car — all of these reveal spending, which is itself only an indirect, noisy signal of underlying financial position, filtered through debt, family help, and personal priorities a viewer can't actually see. A disclosed salary is different: it's a direct, largely unambiguous number, assigned by an identifiable institution, with comparatively little room for the kind of generous reinterpretation a viewer might apply to an ambiguous purchase. That directness is part of why a compensation figure lands so much harder than an equally sized gap inferred from lifestyle alone.

Professional peer comparison operates through several distinct mechanisms, and understanding each one explains both why a single disclosed number can derail an otherwise satisfying career and why the resulting distress so rarely resolves cleanly even once the gap has been addressed.

The foundational mechanism is, once again, rooted in Festinger's social comparison theory, but it's worth naming a specific variant here: research on comparison in workplace and compensation contexts consistently finds that satisfaction with pay is driven far more strongly by relative standing among perceived peers than by the absolute number itself. A raise that would have felt genuinely satisfying in isolation can feel deeply unsatisfying the moment it's learned that a peer received a larger one, and a salary that felt entirely adequate on Tuesday can feel inadequate on Thursday with no change in its actual purchasing power — because pay satisfaction was never really being evaluated against an absolute standard to begin with. It was always being evaluated against a comparison, whether or not the comparison was consciously available yet.

A second mechanism draws directly on economist Erzo Luttmer's substantial empirical research on relative income and well-being: Luttmer's work, using large-scale survey and neighborhood-level income data, found that a person's reported life satisfaction is meaningfully affected not just by their own income, but by the income of others in their immediate reference group — people earning the same amount reported significantly lower well-being when their neighbors or peers earned more, even holding their own actual income constant. This finding matters enormously here because it demonstrates, with real empirical rigor rather than mere plausibility, that relative income genuinely moves the needle on well-being independent of absolute income — which means the man whose Tuesday satisfaction collapsed on Wednesday wasn't being irrational or petty. He was responding to a documented, measurable psychological reality that his own income, unchanged, had become less satisfying purely because a comparison figure had entered his awareness.

A third mechanism deserves careful attention: research on **equity theory**, introduced in the previous chapter's discussion of sibling inheritance, applies with particular sharpness to professional compensation, because workplace compensation is, unlike most financial domains, explicitly framed around inputs and outputs — effort, skill, tenure, contribution — that invite direct, structured comparison in a way a sibling's overall life trajectory does not. When a person perceives their input-to-outcome ratio as lower than a comparable peer's, equity theory predicts a specific, measurable form of distress distinct from ordinary disappointment — a felt sense of injustice, not just insufficiency, which explains why the woman in this chapter's second scene experienced something closer to indignation than plain dissatisfaction once she learned about the gap.

A fourth mechanism is specific to why the distress often persists even after a raise partially closes a discovered gap: research on the **anchoring effect**, already introduced earlier in this book, applies here in a particularly durable way — once a specific comparison figure becomes known, it functions as a fixed anchor against which every future number gets evaluated, including a subsequent raise intended to resolve the original discomfort. A partial raise that closes half the gap doesn't return a person to their pre-disclosure baseline satisfaction. It simply creates a new, smaller gap, still measured against the same anchor, which is part of why "just give them a raise" so rarely fully resolves this pattern once a specific number has genuinely lodged itself in someone's head.

A fifth mechanism worth naming, particularly relevant to the freelance designer's imprecise, inferred comparison: research on **information asymmetry and estimation under uncertainty** describes how, in the absence of reliable, verified data, people tend to fill gaps with impressions gathered from limited, unrepresentative, often self-selected samples — social media posts, industry chatter, the loudest voices in a professional community, who are rarely a random or representative cross-section of actual market rates. The designer's two years of rate anxiety were driven by a comparison sample he never rigorously verified, gathered largely from whichever peers happened to be the most vocal about their own rates — a group that skews, reliably, toward people confident enough to disclose favorable numbers and away from the much larger, quieter population charging less, whose silence never gets weighed into the impression at all.

A sixth mechanism explains why compensation comparisons produce a specific kind of distress that other financial comparisons in this book don't quite match: unlike a peer's house or a peer's vacation, a colleague's salary is frequently understood, correctly or not, as an institutional judgment of relative worth — set by an employer who has access to both people's actual performance and contribution, and who chose, deliberately, to value one more than the other. This institutional framing gives compensation comparison a specific authority that a casually observed lifestyle difference doesn't carry. It doesn't just suggest the other person has more. It implies someone in a position to judge accurately looked at both of you and decided.

There's an seventh mechanism worth adding, specific to why this pattern hits harder inside a single workplace than across separate companies: research on **organizational justice**, extending the equity-theory framework already introduced in this book, distinguishes between distributive justice — whether outcomes themselves feel fair — and procedural justice, already discussed in an earlier chapter — whether the process producing those outcomes feels fair. A pay gap discovered between coworkers inside the same organization implicates both forms of justice simultaneously, because the same employer set both people's pay through the same internal process, using presumably the same criteria. This double violation is part of why an in-house compensation gap tends to produce sharper, more lasting distress than an equivalent gap discovered between two people at entirely different companies, where no single shared process can be blamed for the disparity.

There's a eighth piece worth naming: research on **pay transparency and disclosure norms** across organizational psychology has found that even partial, informal disclosure of compensation information — a slip during a project conversation, an overheard remark — produces measurable shifts in reported job satisfaction that persist for months after the disclosure, considerably longer than comparably sized shifts triggered by non-compensation-related workplace events. Compensation information appears to carry unusual, lasting weight once it enters awareness, distinct from ordinary workplace comparisons about status, recognition, or responsibility, which tend to fade from active attention far more quickly.

What it costs you

The most direct cost is a genuine, measurable erosion of job and career satisfaction that has nothing to do with any actual change in the job itself. This is a real cost, not a trivial one — sustained dissatisfaction driven by peer comparison has been linked, across a substantial body of workplace psychology research, to increased turnover intention, reduced engagement, and lower overall reported well-being, all triggered not by any deterioration in actual working conditions but purely by the disclosure of a comparison figure that would, absent that disclosure, never have affected anything at all.

There's a compounding cost specific to how this pattern distorts career decision-making. A person driven primarily by closing a peer-comparison gap, rather than by a genuinely considered assessment of their own goals, skills, and market position, is prone to making career moves — job changes, negotiation demands, freelance rate increases — calibrated against a number that may itself be inaccurate, unrepresentative, or simply not comparable to their own actual circumstances in ways that matter. Chasing a peer's number rather than your own honestly assessed market value can lead to decisions that look, on paper, like advocacy for yourself, but are functionally closer to a reaction against a comparison that was never verified to begin with.

There's a relational cost within workplaces specifically worth naming: peer comparison, once triggered, tends to color how colleagues relate to each other going forward, introducing a layer of quiet calculation into relationships that previously felt collegial and uncomplicated. The woman who discovered the compensation gap with her coworker may find it genuinely harder, for months or longer, to collaborate with that colleague with the same uncomplicated ease she once did — not because anything changed about the colleague's behavior, but because the comparison, once made real by a specific number, is difficult to fully unknow, coloring interactions that have nothing to do with pay at all.

There's a final cost worth naming, and it points toward a genuine irony at the heart of this pattern: professional peer comparison, precisely because it depends so heavily on incomplete, selectively disclosed information, frequently produces distress calibrated against numbers that aren't actually accurate or representative. A single overheard figure, a friend's possibly exaggerated account, an unusually favorable outlier within a professional community — all of these can trigger genuine, lasting career dissatisfaction while resting on data no more reliable than a rumor. The cost, in these cases, is paid in full regardless of whether the comparison that triggered it was even true.

There's a cost worth naming that touches specifically on how compensation comparison shapes a person's willingness to stay in a genuinely good job. A role that offers real meaning, real flexibility, real learning, and a fair, if not spectacular, salary can become suddenly intolerable the moment a peer comparison surfaces, even though nothing about the actual balance of what the job offers has changed. This can push people out of positions that were, on every dimension besides the comparison itself, serving them well — a decision that looks, from the outside, like reasonable self-advocacy, but that was actually driven by a single number's sudden appearance rather than any real, considered reassessment of the whole picture.

There's a cost worth naming that's specific to how peer compensation comparison affects collaboration and mentorship within a team. A colleague who has learned, even informally, that they're paid less than a peer doing comparable work may become less willing to offer that peer genuine support, cover for them during a difficult stretch, or advocate for their ideas in a meeting — not out of any conscious decision to withhold goodwill, but because the discovered gap quietly recolors the relationship from collegial partnership toward something closer to competition, a shift that can measurably reduce the quality of collaboration on a team without ever being named directly by anyone involved.

There's a cost worth naming that shows up specifically over the course of a career rather than any single job. A person who repeatedly changes jobs primarily in reaction to disclosed peer compensation, rather than as part of a genuinely considered career strategy, can end up with a resume shaped more by other people's numbers than by their own coherent professional direction — a pattern that, ironically, can itself become a disadvantage in future compensation negotiations, where a clear, purposeful narrative about career growth tends to carry more weight than a series of moves that, examined honestly, were mostly reactions to what someone else happened to be paid.

The overrides

Give yourself a fixed, brief mourning period for a discovered gap, and set an end date for it. A day or two of genuine frustration is a reasonable response to real information. Deciding, in advance, roughly how long you're willing to let that frustration run before shifting into either direct action or genuine acceptance keeps the discovery from settling into the kind of indefinite, low-grade resentment that quietly damages a colleague relationship for months without ever being addressed directly.

Seek out real, aggregated compensation data before trusting a single disclosed or inferred number. Structured, broad-based salary data — industry surveys, aggregated compensation reports, verified sources covering a genuine sample rather than a handful of vocal peers — gives a far more reliable picture than any single overheard figure, and is considerably less likely to trigger distress based on an unrepresentative outlier.

When a specific comparison figure triggers distress, separate the question of fairness from the question of satisfaction, explicitly. "Is this actually inequitable, based on real, comparable inputs" is a different, more answerable question than "does this number make me feel worse than I did an hour ago" — and only the first one should actually drive a career decision.

If you decide a gap is real and worth addressing, address it directly rather than letting it operate as background resentment. A calm, specific conversation with a manager, grounded in your own actual contributions rather than someone else's disclosed number, is far more likely to produce a durable resolution than private rumination — which, as this chapter's mechanism section makes clear, tends to persist even after a partial fix.

Build your own sense of fair compensation from your own criteria, before a comparison figure arrives to distort it. Knowing, in advance, what you consider fair compensation for your specific skills, contributions, and market position gives you a stable reference point to evaluate any future disclosed number against — rather than letting whichever number happens to arrive first set the terms of the entire conversation.

Notice how quickly satisfaction with your own compensation recovers, or doesn't, after a comparison figure fades from immediate memory. If dissatisfaction persists well past the point where the triggering event feels emotionally current, that's useful information that the underlying issue may be broader than the single comparison — worth examining directly rather than continuing to relitigate against one specific peer's number.

A closing script, for the moment a colleague's or peer's compensation figure lands: "That's information about them. My worth isn't set by comparison — it's set by what I actually bring and what I've actually decided is fair." Say it plainly, even if the sting doesn't fully disappear right away. The sentence isn't meant to erase the feeling instantly. It's meant to keep the feeling from making a decision on your behalf before you've had a chance to evaluate it clearly.

Write down your own career narrative in a single paragraph, updated once a year, independent of any comparison. A clear, self-authored account of what you're building and why gives you a stable reference point to test every future job change or negotiation against — including the ones triggered by a peer's disclosed number — so the decision gets evaluated against your own direction rather than only against the comparison that prompted it.

When negotiating compensation, lead with your own documented contribution rather than a peer's disclosed number. A case built on your own specific results tends to land better with decision-makers than one built on comparison, and it also protects you from anchoring your own sense of fair value to a figure that, as this chapter has shown, may not even be accurate.

If a compensation gap with a specific colleague is affecting how you collaborate with them, name that shift to yourself explicitly before it hardens into habit. Recognizing "I've been less generous with this person since I learned about the gap" is often enough to consciously restore the collaboration, even while the underlying compensation question is still being addressed separately through the appropriate channel.

The rule to remember: your paycheck didn't get worse the moment you learned someone else's — your comparison point did, and only one of those two things is actually worth acting on.

Chapter 8 — The Curated Peer

Why the People You Measure Yourself Against Were Never a Random Sample

She could tell you, without hesitation, roughly how a dozen people she's never met in person are doing financially — a rotating handful of accounts she follows, people whose homes, vacations, and milestone purchases she's watched accumulate for years through a screen, in a relationship so one-directional and so quietly persistent that she rarely stops to notice how strange it actually is. She couldn't tell you nearly as much about several actual friends from her own daily life, people she talks to regularly, whose real financial situations she has genuine, current context for. The dozen strangers are more vivid to her, more present in her sense of what a good financial life looks like, than the people she actually knows — because the dozen strangers show up constantly, curated, polished, presented in exactly the light each of them chose, while her real friends show up the way real people show up: complicated, mixed, occasionally telling her about a hard month, rarely photographing the good ones for an audience.

She has never once stopped to ask whether these dozen people are a representative sample of anything. They aren't, and on some level she knows they aren't — she knows, intellectually, that people who post about their financial lives skew heavily toward people whose financial lives currently look good, and skew even further toward people whose entire livelihood depends on appearing to be doing exceptionally well. And yet the knowing doesn't fully protect her from the felt experience of exposure — hundreds of small, repeated glimpses into a version of financial life edited for maximum impressiveness, absorbed so continuously that it has quietly become her ambient sense of normal, regardless of how thoroughly she'd disavow that if asked directly.

A different version of the same mechanism operates without any screen involved at all. A man who works in a specific, high-earning niche of his industry has structured his entire professional and social life, without ever quite deciding to, around people who work in that same high-earning niche — conferences, professional associations, a social circle that formed almost entirely through work. His sense of what constitutes a normal, adequate income has been built almost exclusively from this narrow, unrepresentative slice of his actual broader industry, most of which earns considerably less than the specific niche he happens to occupy. He feels, most years, unremarkable, ordinary, solidly mid-pack — a feeling produced entirely by a comparison sample that would look, to almost anyone outside his specific professional bubble, like a group of considerable outliers.

A third scene plays out through inheritance of proximity rather than active selection: a woman who grew up in a modest household moved, as an adult, into a neighborhood considerably more affluent than the one she grew up in, for reasons that had nothing to do with financial comparison — good schools, a manageable commute, a house she and her husband could technically afford with a stretch. Years later, her sense of financial normalcy is calibrated almost entirely against neighbors she never chose as a comparison group and wouldn't describe, if asked directly, as people she measures herself against at all — and yet her ongoing, low-grade sense of relative financial inadequacy tracks, with striking consistency, the specific affluence of the specific block she happens to live on, a comparison sample selected entirely by a real estate decision made for entirely different reasons years earlier.

What's actually happening

It's worth being specific about the difference between this chapter's pattern and ordinary trajectory comparison covered earlier in this book, because the two can feel similar from the inside but operate through different channels. A trajectory check compares against people you actually know, with real, if incomplete, context about their lives. The curated peer pattern compares against people, or a social tier, encountered with almost no context at all — a single visible slice, repeated often enough to feel substantial, standing in for an entire life you know almost nothing else about. The thinner the actual information, paradoxically, the more room there is for the comparison to feel total and overwhelming, because there's no inconvenient complicating detail available to interrupt it.

The mechanism underlying this pattern has a name that predates any current technology, though it operates now with a scale and continuity that would have been unimaginable to earlier generations: research on **selective exposure**, a foundational concept in media and social psychology, describes how people's information environments are shaped by systematic, often invisible selection processes — some chosen deliberately, many simply inherited from circumstance — that reliably skew what a person sees toward specific, unrepresentative slices of a much broader, more varied reality.

The first and most important piece of this mechanism is what researchers studying self-presentation call **positive self-presentation bias** — extending directly from Erving Goffman's foundational work on impression management, already introduced earlier in this book, and specifically documented in research on how people present themselves in settings where an audience is aware they're being observed. People disclose their financial successes far more readily and far more visibly than their financial struggles, across essentially every social context studied — in casual conversation, in professional settings, and especially in any setting explicitly built around presenting a curated version of oneself to an audience. This creates a systematic, structural skew in the sample of financial lives any person is likely to observe: the visible data points reliably overrepresent success and reliably underrepresent difficulty, not because struggle is rare, but because struggle is disclosed far less willingly than success.

A second mechanism comes from research on **survivorship bias**, a concept with roots in statistics and made broadly famous through analyses in fields ranging from finance to military engineering, describes the systematic error of drawing conclusions from a visible, "surviving" sample while ignoring the much larger, invisible sample that didn't make it into view at all. The dozen accounts the woman in this chapter's opening scene follows are, functionally, financial survivors — people whose situations currently look impressive enough to be worth broadcasting. The much larger population of people whose finances look ordinary, difficult, or simply unremarkable enough not to be worth sharing never enters her sample at all, which means her sense of "normal" is built entirely from a systematically unrepresentative slice of reality, skewed in one predictable direction every single time.

A third mechanism deserves careful attention, and it explains why proximity-based comparison — the neighborhood scene, the professional-niche scene — operates just as powerfully as any curated, chosen comparison: research on **contextual and neighborhood effects** within social and economic psychology has documented that people's sense of relative economic standing is shaped significantly by the specific, local comparison context they happen to inhabit, largely independent of their actual broader position. A person can be genuinely affluent by any national or even regional standard and still feel persistently behind, purely because their specific neighborhood, workplace, or professional niche happens to sit at the high end of that broader distribution — a mismatch between actual position and felt position produced entirely by an unchosen, structurally skewed comparison context.

There's a fourth mechanism worth adding, specific to sustained, repeated exposure over time: research on the **mere exposure effect**, developed substantially by psychologist Robert Zajonc, describes how repeated exposure to a stimulus increases familiarity with it and, over time, shifts a person's baseline sense of what counts as normal or expected. Continuous, repeated exposure to a specific, curated slice of financial life — whether through a screen, a workplace, or a neighborhood — doesn't just provide occasional data points for comparison. It gradually recalibrates the entire baseline against which "normal" gets measured, through sheer accumulated repetition, regardless of how unrepresentative that specific slice actually is of the broader population it's silently standing in for.

A fifth mechanism worth naming: research on **algorithmic curation and engagement optimization**, a growing area of study within media psychology, has documented that systems designed to maximize engagement tend to systematically surface content that provokes strong reactions — including content depicting notable financial success or notable financial extremity — at rates considerably higher than that content's actual prevalence in the broader population would justify. This compounds the underlying selective-exposure and survivorship-bias mechanisms already at work, adding a further, largely invisible layer of skew on top of an already unrepresentative sample, without the person doing the comparing ever having consciously selected for any of it.

A sixth mechanism explains why this pattern is so specifically hard to correct even for people who understand statistics reasonably well in other areas of life: research on **base rate neglect**, well documented across judgment and decision-making studies since the early work of Kahneman and Tversky, describes how people consistently underweight general, population-level information in favor of specific, vivid, individual cases, even when the general information is demonstrably more reliable. Knowing, abstractly, that most people don't live like the curated sample you follow rarely overrides the vivid, specific, repeatedly reinforced impression the sample itself produces — the base rate loses to the vivid case almost every time, which is precisely the finding base rate neglect research keeps confirming across entirely unrelated domains.

There's an seventh mechanism worth adding, because it explains why the curated sample tends to feel more emotionally present than statistics or reasoned argument ever quite manage to: research on **narrative transportation** within media psychology describes how a vivid, story-shaped piece of information — a specific person's specific milestone, told with real detail — engages attention and emotional investment far more powerfully than an equivalent piece of abstract, statistical information, even when the statistical information is objectively more representative and more reliable. A single curated post showing one person's new house will, almost every time, out-compete a demographically accurate statistic about typical homeownership rates for the emotional real estate it occupies in a viewer's mind, regardless of which one actually describes reality more accurately.

There's a eighth piece worth adding, specific to why the professional-niche and neighborhood versions of this pattern are especially resistant to correction: because these comparison samples are embedded in a person's actual daily life rather than encountered through a screen, there's no obvious "close the app" intervention available to interrupt them. A curated online sample can, at least in principle, be muted or unfollowed. A neighborhood or a professional community that quietly sets the local standard for "normal" is considerably harder to simply opt out of, since doing so would mean changing where you live or who you work alongside — which means this version of the pattern often has to be managed through deliberate reframing rather than removal, a genuinely harder task.

What it costs you

The most direct cost is a persistently miscalibrated sense of financial normalcy, applied to real decisions with real consequences — how much to save, what standard of living to expect, what risk to take in pursuit of a lifestyle that was never actually representative of how most people, even most people in a similar income bracket, are genuinely living. Decisions calibrated against a systematically skewed sample tend to be systematically poor decisions, not because the person making them lacks judgment, but because the input feeding that judgment was never a fair sample to begin with.

There's a compounding cost specific to how this pattern generates a chronic, low-grade sense of inadequacy that resists correction even when directly confronted with accurate information. Knowing, intellectually, that a curated sample is unrepresentative — as the woman in this chapter's opening scene does know — turns out to be far less protective than most people assume, because the mere exposure effect and the accumulated weight of repeated impressions operate below the level of conscious belief. You can hold the correct fact in your head — this sample is skewed — and still feel the skewed sample's emotional effect in full, because knowing a bias exists and being immune to it are two entirely different things, and only the first one comes easily.

There's a cost specific to how this pattern erodes the value of genuinely accurate information available elsewhere in a person's life. The woman who could recite a dozen strangers' apparent financial trajectories but knew far less about her actual friends' real situations has, in effect, let an unrepresentative, curated sample crowd out a more honest, more available, more genuinely useful one — the real, complicated, mixed financial lives of people she actually knows well enough to have accurate context about, sitting right alongside her, largely ignored in favor of a more vivid but less trustworthy comparison set.

There's a final cost worth naming, and it belongs specifically to the neighborhood and professional-niche versions of this pattern: because these comparison samples were never consciously chosen for comparison purposes at all — they were inherited from an unrelated decision about where to live or what career to pursue — the resulting sense of relative inadequacy can feel especially disorienting and especially hard to trace back to its actual source. A person can spend years feeling vaguely behind without ever identifying that the feeling is being produced almost entirely by an accident of geography or professional circumstance, rather than by anything meaningfully true about their actual financial position.

There's a cost worth naming that touches specifically on how a skewed comparison sample shapes a person's expectations for their own children or future self. A parent whose sense of normal has been quietly recalibrated by a curated or proximity-based sample may set expectations — for a child's education, for a family's lifestyle, for what a "responsible" adult life should include — that reflect the unrepresentative sample rather than any honest assessment of what's actually sustainable or necessary. These expectations, once set, tend to outlive the specific comparison that produced them, carried forward as if they were independently arrived-at values rather than the residue of an unrepresentative sample encountered years earlier.

There's a cost worth naming that's specific to how a persistently skewed comparison sample affects a person's willingness to talk honestly with anyone about their own real financial life. If the ambient standard has quietly become an unrepresentative, success-skewed sample, admitting to an ordinary, honest financial reality can start to feel like a confession rather than simply a fact — which discourages exactly the kind of frank, accurate conversation that would otherwise help recalibrate the skewed baseline back toward something real. The distortion, left unaddressed, tends to reinforce its own silence.

There's a cost worth naming that runs specifically through decisions about lifestyle spending rather than saving or investing. A person whose baseline sense of normal has been quietly recalibrated by a curated or proximity-based sample tends to experience ordinary, previously satisfying choices — a modest car, a standard vacation, an unremarkable home — as somehow lacking, not because anything about those choices changed, but because the comparison sample shifted what "unremarkable" means. This can drive real, measurable increases in spending aimed at closing a gap that was never accurately measured in the first place, chasing a version of normal that the actual, broader population the person belongs to was never living anyway.

The overrides

Take a genuine break from your primary comparison environment periodically, and pay attention to what your sense of "enough" does in its absence. A week away from the usual feed, neighborhood routine, or professional circle, spent instead in a genuinely different context, often reveals just how much of your baseline sense of normal was being propped up by continuous exposure rather than anything you'd independently choose if starting fresh.

Deliberately audit your comparison sample for representativeness, at least once. List the specific people, accounts, or groups currently shaping your sense of financial normalcy, and ask honestly what kind of sample they actually represent — a curated, self-selected, success-skewed sample, or something closer to a genuine, representative cross-section. Naming the skew explicitly is usually enough to loosen its grip on your baseline sense of normal.

When a curated success story triggers a spending decision, wait through one full pay cycle before acting on it. The specific urgency a curated comparison produces tends to fade considerably within a few weeks, once the vivid original impression has had time to compete with the accumulated, quieter reality of your own ordinary days — a delay that costs nothing and reliably filters out the decisions that were never really about your own needs to begin with.

Deliberately seek out and weight the invisible, unrepresented population. For every curated success story that shapes your sense of normal, deliberately remind yourself of the much larger, much less visible population who never got mentioned or shown — people managing debt, people whose situations look ordinary, people who never had a reason to broadcast anything. You don't need direct access to their stories to remember, reliably, that this larger population exists and dramatically outnumbers the curated sample you're actually seeing.

Weight the real, accurate information already available to you from people you actually know. Deliberately prioritize what you genuinely know about close friends' and family members' real financial lives — the complicated, mixed, honest version — over the more vivid but less trustworthy impressions gathered from a curated or proximity-based sample. Accurate, if less exciting, information should carry more weight in shaping your sense of normal than vivid, unrepresentative information, even though the vivid version tends to feel more present and more real.

If a specific comparison context — a neighborhood, a professional niche, a particular circle — was inherited rather than chosen, name that inheritance explicitly. Recognizing that your comparison sample was selected by a housing decision, a career path, or simple proximity, rather than by any deliberate choice to measure yourself against these specific people, helps separate the feeling of relative standing from any actual, meaningful verdict on your financial life.

Periodically step outside your usual comparison environment on purpose, and notice how your sense of "normal" shifts. A visit to a different city, a conversation with someone from a genuinely different economic context, a deliberate look at broader, aggregated data — any of these can recalibrate a sense of normal that's quietly narrowed to fit an unrepresentative local sample, restoring a wider, more accurate frame of reference.

A closing script, for the moment a curated or proximity-based comparison starts shaping your sense of adequacy: "This is a sample, not a census — and it was never built to be fair." Say it plainly, and let it do the work of reminding you that what you're seeing was selected, filtered, and skewed long before it ever reached you, by forces that had nothing to do with representing reality accurately.

Actively seek out one honest, unfiltered account of an ordinary financial life for every curated one you encounter. A frank conversation with a trusted friend about real numbers, a genuine account of an unremarkable year, does more to restore an accurate baseline than any amount of reasoning about statistics in the abstract — because it gives the base rate a vivid, memorable case of its own to compete with.

Curate your own inputs the way you'd curate any other information diet. Just as you'd limit exposure to a source that reliably produced bad decisions in any other domain, treat a comparison sample that reliably produces financial anxiety or poor decisions as worth deliberately reducing exposure to — not out of denial, but out of the same ordinary self-protection you'd apply to any other consistently unreliable source of information.

Be the honest account yourself, at least occasionally, with someone you trust. Sharing an ordinary, unremarkable financial year out loud does more than protect you from your own skewed samples — it helps correct someone else's, breaking a small piece of the silence this pattern depends on to keep spreading.

The rule to remember: the people you measure yourself against were almost never chosen for their representativeness — they were chosen by an algorithm, a curated feed, a neighborhood, or a niche, and none of those were ever built to show you a fair sample of how people are actually doing.

Chapter 9 — The Wrong Decade

Why Comparing Your Progress to a Life That Ran on Different Rules Always Leaves You Short

Her father bought his first house at twenty-six, on a single income, in a job that required no advanced degree and came with a pension he could count on decades later, a pension that still, to this day, forms the backbone of his retirement. She is thirty-four, holds an advanced degree her father's generation would have considered remarkable, works harder by any honest measure than he ever had to, and does not yet own a home — a fact that sits in her, most days, not as a neutral difference in circumstance but as a specific, personal shortfall, a sense that she should have gotten further by now than she actually has. Her father, without any unkindness in it at all, sometimes reinforces the comparison directly — a comment about how he'd managed to buy a house "at your age," delivered as gentle encouragement, landing as something closer to an indictment of a decade she didn't choose to be born into.

The comparison feels, from inside it, like a fair one. Same family, same values around hard work, same basic life stages —

degree, job, marriage, house — arriving in the same rough sequence. What the comparison doesn't account for, because it was never built to account for it, is that the two of them are running the exact same race on tracks that no longer resemble each other in any way that actually matters: a housing market that has grown, in real terms, dramatically more expensive relative to income since her father's twenties; a job market that, in her specific field, virtually requires the advanced degree that cost her years and real money her father's generation, in a different economy, simply didn't need to spend; a labor market that no longer routinely offers the kind of stable, pension-backed employment her father's generation could reasonably expect to find without unusual difficulty. None of these are excuses in the sense of things that don't matter. They're the actual conditions of the race, and the race her father ran was, in ways neither of them has ever sat down and actually calculated, a genuinely different and genuinely easier one.

A different version of the same mismatch plays out generationally in the opposite direction. A man in his late fifties watches his adult children navigate a job market and housing market considerably harder than the one he came up in, and finds himself, with real and generous intentions, offering financial comparisons meant to be reassuring — "it took me a while too" — that don't actually hold up under any real scrutiny, because the "while" it took him unfolded under conditions substantially more forgiving than the ones his children are actually facing. His intentions are good. The comparison itself, however kindly meant, quietly implies that his children's slower progress reflects something about their effort or choices rather than something about the two very different economic environments each generation happened to inherit.

A third scene plays out without any generational gap at all, just a mismatched set of starting conditions mistaken for a level playing field. Two friends, the same age, graduated the same year, compare their financial progress as though they'd run identical races — without either of them ever explicitly accounting for the fact that one entered the workforce during a genuine boom year for their shared industry, while the other graduated directly into a downturn that measurably and lastingly suppressed early-career earnings for an entire cohort, a documented effect that had nothing to do with either person's talent, effort, or choices, and everything to do with the specific, arbitrary timing of when each of them happened to finish school.

What's actually happening

It's worth naming why this particular comparison so often escapes scrutiny even in families that are otherwise thoughtful and self-aware about money. Every other pattern in this book involves two people living, at least roughly, in the same economic moment — the comparison might be unfair for other reasons, but the ground beneath both people is at least the same ground. A cross-generational comparison quietly assumes a shared ground that was never actually there, which means the unfairness runs deeper than in any other pattern this book describes, and yet is somehow the least visible of all of them, precisely because "hard work leads to reward" is such a comforting, well-worn story that almost nobody stops to check whether the rules of the game were actually the same for both players.

The mechanism at the heart of this pattern is, in some ways, the simplest of any covered in this book, and also one of the most persistently overlooked: a comparison that ignores a genuine, measurable difference in starting conditions isn't actually a comparison of two people's choices or effort at all. It's a comparison of two different economic environments, dressed up as a comparison of character.

Economist Richard Easterlin's research on relative income and life satisfaction, and the substantial body of work it inspired, established early on that people evaluate their economic position relative to a reference standard rather than in absolute terms — a foundational finding this book has returned to repeatedly. What's specifically relevant here is a less-discussed extension of that same insight: the reference standard people use often includes an inherited, internalized sense of what a "normal" life trajectory should look like, absorbed from parents, from broader cultural narratives about hard work and reward, from an earlier era's genuinely different economic conditions — a standard that, once internalized, doesn't automatically update itself to reflect a substantially changed economic environment, even when the environment has, in fact, substantially changed.

A second mechanism draws on documented labor economics research into what's sometimes called **cohort effects** or **scarring effects** — a well-established finding, replicated across multiple economic downturns and multiple countries, that people who enter the labor market during a recession experience measurably lower earnings that persist for years, sometimes decades, after the downturn ends, compared to similarly qualified peers who happened to graduate during stronger economic conditions. This is not a difference in talent, effort, or choices. It's a documented, structural effect of timing, and it means the friend who graduated into a downturn in this chapter's third scene is not, in any meaningful sense, running the same race as the friend who graduated into a boom — however identical their degrees, their intelligence, and their work ethic actually were.

A third mechanism deserves careful attention: the same **reference point** and **anchoring** dynamics introduced in earlier chapters, drawing on Kahneman and Tversky's research, apply here with a specific generational twist. A parent's own life trajectory, observed closely and admiringly throughout childhood, functions as a deeply anchored reference point for what a "normal" adult life should look like — installed early, reinforced over decades of observation, and almost never explicitly updated to account for how dramatically the underlying economic conditions have shifted between the parent's twenties and the child's. The daughter in this chapter's opening scene isn't comparing herself against an abstract, chosen standard. She's comparing herself against a reference point installed in childhood, under economic conditions that no longer exist, using rules that quietly stopped applying without anyone formally announcing the change.

A fourth mechanism explains why this particular comparison resists correction even once the underlying economic differences are pointed out directly: research on the **just-world hypothesis**, developed substantially by social psychologist Melvin Lerner, describes a well-documented tendency for people to believe, often at a barely conscious level, that outcomes are generally deserved — that hard work generally leads to proportional reward, and that a shortfall in outcome generally reflects a shortfall in effort or ability rather than an external, structural cause. This belief, comforting in many contexts because it makes the world feel orderly and controllable, becomes specifically distorting when applied to cross-generational or cross-cohort financial comparison, because it pulls both the comparer and the person being compared toward attributing a structural, economy-wide difference to something personal and internal instead — the father's gentle "at your age" comment isn't malicious; it's the just-world hypothesis operating quietly in the background, making a structural difference feel, to both of them, like a personal one.

A fifth mechanism worth naming: economic research on **housing affordability trends** and **wage-to-cost-of-living ratios** across recent decades has documented substantial, measurable shifts in the relationship between typical entry-level wages and typical major life-purchase costs — home prices relative to median income, in particular, have moved in well-documented, statistically significant ways across many regions over the timeframe separating most parents' early adulthoods from their children's. This isn't a matter of perception or generational complaint. It's a measurable, citable economic reality, and comparisons that ignore it aren't measuring effort or character at all. They're measuring, unknowingly, the difference between two economic eras and mislabeling the result as a difference between two people.

A sixth mechanism explains why this pattern is so specifically hard to correct within a family even once the structural data is on the table: research on **narrative identity** within personality psychology describes how people construct a coherent life story out of their own remembered experience, and how that story, once formed, tends to be defended against information that would require revising it substantially. A parent's account of "working hard and buying a house at twenty-six" is not simply a data point to that parent. It's load-bearing within a lifelong personal narrative about effort and reward, which means presenting the parent with structural housing-cost data doesn't just correct a fact — it asks the parent to revise a story they've been telling about their own life for decades, a request considerably harder to fully absorb than the data itself would suggest.

There's an seventh mechanism worth adding, and it points toward why this particular comparison is so worth naming explicitly as its own chapter rather than folding into the earlier trajectory or milestone chapters: every other comparison in this book at least theoretically involves two people operating under the same rules at the same time. This one doesn't. The daughter and her father are not, and never were, running the same race under the same conditions, which means no amount of individual effort on her part could have fully closed the gap the comparison implies she should be able to close. Naming this distinction matters because it changes what "fixing" the comparison actually looks like — not working harder to match an outcome that was calibrated for a different track, but building an honest, separate standard for the actual track underfoot.

There's a eighth piece worth adding, specific to the peer version of this pattern rather than the generational one: research on **survivorship and hindsight bias** in career and economic outcomes describes how, once an economic downturn has passed, its effects tend to be remembered as less severe and less structurally determined than they actually were at the time, because the visible survivors of that period — the people whose careers ultimately recovered — are more available to memory than the considerably larger population whose earnings never fully caught back up. This means even the two friends in this chapter's third scene, looking back years later, may both underestimate how much of their earnings gap was genuinely structural, each instead defaulting, gradually, to the more comfortable, less examined explanation that the gap must simply reflect something about each of their individual choices.

What it costs you

The most direct cost is a persistent, often deeply internalized sense of personal inadequacy attached to an outcome that was never actually within the compared person's full control. The daughter in this chapter's opening scene isn't behind because she made worse choices than her father — she's navigating a housing market and a labor market that are, by well-documented economic measures, genuinely harder to succeed in by the standard her father's generation set. Attributing that gap to personal shortfall rather than structural difference produces real, unearned distress, and can drive genuinely poor decisions in response — taking on excessive debt to force a milestone that made economic sense in a different decade, or abandoning a genuinely sound, patient financial strategy out of a mistaken belief that a faster peer's or parent's pace should have been achievable.

There's a compounding cost specific to how cross-generational comparison distorts family relationships, often in ways neither generation intends. A well-meaning parent's comparison, offered as encouragement, can land as quiet judgment; a struggling adult child's private sense of inadequacy, left unexamined and unspoken, can produce a specific, hard-to-name resentment toward a parent who never intended to cause it, built from a comparison that neither of them ever sat down to actually stress-test against the real economic data available to correct it.

There's a cost worth naming that runs in the opposite direction as well: parents who compare their own harder circumstances against a child's relatively easier ones — a phenomenon that occurs just as often as the reverse, depending on which specific decade and which specific economic conditions happen to be under comparison — can produce a different but related distortion, minimizing genuine, structural difficulty a younger generation is facing by measuring it against a different era's different, and not necessarily lesser, set of challenges. The mechanism runs in both directions; the cost of ignoring genuine cohort differences is the same regardless of which generation happens to come out looking better in the mismatched comparison.

There's a final cost worth naming, and it belongs to peer comparisons within the same generation as much as across generations: when cohort effects like recession-era earning scars go unrecognized, a person who graduated into unlucky timing can spend years attributing a real, structural, well-documented earnings gap to a personal failing — a specific, compounding form of self-blame layered on top of an already difficult economic hand, made considerably worse by a comparison against a same-age peer whose only real advantage was the arbitrary timing of a diploma.

There's a cost worth naming that touches specifically on how the wrong-decade comparison affects a person's willingness to feel proud of genuinely hard-won progress. Someone navigating a measurably harder economic environment than their parent's and still managing real, steady progress — a smaller but growing savings account, a stable if modest career, debt paid down against real headwinds — often can't quite let themselves feel proud of it, because the comparison against an earlier, easier decade keeps recasting real accomplishment as mere adequacy at best. This is, in a very real sense, a theft of earned pride, and it's one of the more quietly damaging costs in this entire book, because the person paying it is often doing everything right and still can't feel it.

There's a cost worth naming that's specific to how this comparison, left unexamined, can quietly shape a family's advice-giving across an entire generation. A parent who never updates their own reference point for what a "normal" pace of financial progress looks like will keep offering advice calibrated to a track that no longer exists, and an adult child who never names the mismatch directly will keep receiving that advice as though it were still applicable, absorbing a mild but real erosion of confidence each time a well-meant suggestion doesn't quite fit the actual conditions of the life it's being applied to.

There's a cost worth naming that runs specifically through major, once-in-a-lifetime financial decisions rather than ongoing anxiety. A person measuring their own progress against a parent's or an older peer's genuinely easier decade can be pushed toward decisions that made sense under the earlier era's conditions but carry real, disproportionate risk under current ones — stretching to buy a home at a price-to-income ratio that would have been unremarkable a generation ago but represents genuine financial strain now, or taking on debt to pursue a milestone whose original cost-benefit calculation no longer holds. The comparison doesn't just produce an unfair feeling. It can drive a genuinely unsound decision, made in service of catching up to a target that was calculated under rules that no longer apply.

The overrides

Ask an older relative to describe their own early financial life in specific, concrete detail rather than in the compressed, tidy version that usually gets told. The full version — the help nobody mentions, the stretch of real luck, the cost of living that's been quietly forgotten — is almost always more complicated and more structurally advantaged than the short version, and hearing the long version, once, tends to do more to dissolve an unfair comparison than any amount of data gathered independently.

Actively research the real, documented economic conditions of the era you're comparing against, rather than relying on memory or impression. Housing-price-to-income ratios, typical entry-level wages adjusted for inflation, and cohort-specific labor market data are publicly available and specific enough to replace a vague, unexamined sense that "it was easier back then" with an actual, citable picture of exactly how and how much conditions have shifted — turning a fuzzy, demoralizing comparison into a precise, depersonalized one.

When a cross-generational or cross-cohort comparison surfaces, explicitly separate the structural variable from the

personal one. Ask directly: how much of this gap is explained by a documented, external, economy-wide shift, and how much is genuinely about individual choices? Most honest audits of this question find the structural share considerably larger than the internalized version of the comparison ever assumed.

Notice whether your own family's version of "responsible" and "successful" was ever explicitly defined, or simply inherited without discussion. Many families operate for generations on an unstated, unexamined definition of what counts as doing well financially — naming that definition out loud, once, as a family, and asking whether everyone actually agrees with it, can do more to defuse a running scoreboard than any individual override attempted alone.

If you're the one offering a comparison — as a parent, an older relative, an established peer — actively check the comparison against real data before offering it, even gently, as encouragement. A well-intentioned "it took me a while too" is only genuinely reassuring if the "while" in question unfolded under comparable conditions; offered without that check, it risks landing as quiet judgment rather than the comfort it was meant to be.

Build your own timeline expectations from your own actual economic conditions, not an inherited one. A financial plan and a sense of "on track" built from your own real income, your own region's real housing costs, and your own field's real trajectory will always be a sounder, less demoralizing foundation than one imported from a parent's, an older sibling's, or an earlier peer's genuinely different decade.

Where the structural difference is real and significant, say so plainly, out loud, especially within families. "I know it's hard not to compare, and I also want us both to remember the actual numbers were different when you started out" is a sentence that can defuse decades of quiet, unexamined comparison in a single honest conversation, without requiring anyone to disown genuine hard work on either side of it.

A closing script, for the moment a cross-era comparison surfaces, from either direction: "We didn't run the same race. Comparing the finish times doesn't tell us as much as it feels like it does." Say it to yourself, or say it out loud in the family conversation where it belongs. Either way, it interrupts a comparison that was never actually measuring what it felt like it was measuring.

Before making a major financial decision aimed at "catching up" to an earlier era's or an earlier peer's milestone, run the decision against your own current numbers alone, with the comparison temporarily set aside entirely. If the decision still makes sense once it's evaluated purely on your own current income, costs, and timeline, it may well be sound. If it only makes sense as a way of matching someone else's different-decade outcome, that's worth knowing before, not after, the decision is made.

If you're receiving advice that doesn't seem to fit your actual conditions, say so plainly and specifically, without needing to relitigate the entire relationship to do it. "That worked under different conditions than the ones I'm actually facing" respects the advice-giver's genuine experience while still declining to measure yourself against a track that no longer exists.

If you're offering advice across a generational gap, check your own advice against current data before giving it. A parent or older relative who takes the small extra step of verifying that their well-intentioned guidance still fits current conditions gives that guidance a real chance of being useful, rather than accurate only to a decade that's already over.

The rule to remember: comparing your progress against a life that ran on different economic rules will always leave you feeling short, because you were never actually behind — you were running a different, harder race, and no amount of effort changes the track underneath your feet.

Before You Go

You have now stood in nine rooms. A dinner table where a decade of updates gets silently ranked before the coffee arrives. A goalpost that keeps relocating exactly as fast as you approach it. A friend's lucky stock, quietly rewriting a plan you built with real care. A number in the shower that nobody can trace to an actual calculation. A family scoreboard that never got named, running since childhood, still deciding how an estate gets fought over decades later. The strange relief of measuring yourself against someone doing worse, and what that relief lets you avoid. A paycheck that felt fine on Tuesday and wrong on Thursday, for no reason but a number someone else happened to mention. A curated sample of other people's best days, mistaken for a fair picture of how anyone is actually doing. And a race run against a decade that no longer exists, compared as though the track had never changed underneath either runner's feet.

Different rooms, same architecture underneath all of them. In every one, a financial decision that should have been evaluated on its own terms — your own goals, your own timeline, your own honestly assessed circumstances — got quietly outsourced instead to a number that belonged to somebody else, chosen not because it was the fairest or most useful measure available, but because it happened to be the one standing closest when the moment to decide arrived.

Here is the thesis once more, plainly, the way it was offered at the start: your financial decisions are shaped less by what you actually want than by an ongoing, mostly unconscious scoreboard against people you never agreed to compete with, and the scoreboard runs whether or not you ever look at it on purpose. Nobody in these nine chapters chose their scoreboard deliberately. A friend group formed by accident of geography and timing became a lifelong reference point. A neighborhood chosen for its schools became a silent measure of adequacy. A single overheard number became an anchor that outlasted the conversation that produced it by years. None of these scoreboards were built on purpose. All of them kept running anyway, quietly influencing decisions their owners would have sworn, if you'd asked them directly, were made purely on the merits.

If you recognized yourself as someone whose sense of "enough" keeps moving no matter how much ground you cover, the hardest thing this book can tell you is also the most useful: the moving target was never a sign that you weren't working hard enough, or wanting the right things, or making good decisions. It was a sign that the standard you were measuring against was never actually fixed to begin with — assembled instead from whoever happened to be nearby, updated continuously, upward, by a mechanism that has nothing to do with your own genuine progress and everything to do with proximity. That's not a character flaw. It's what an unexamined comparison instinct does, in every life it's allowed to run unchecked in, and it will keep doing it until someone stops to actually look at where the target came from.

If you recognized yourself instead as someone who's found real, if temporary, relief in comparing downward, the hardest thing this book can tell you is different, but no less important: that relief was genuine, and it was never the same thing as evidence you were actually fine. A feeling produced by comparison and a fact produced by your own real numbers are not interchangeable, however much the first one can be made to stand in for the second when the second one is uncomfortable to look at directly. The work ahead isn't to stop ever feeling that relief. It's to stop letting the relief do the job that only an honest look at your own numbers can actually do.

It's worth pausing, before closing this book, on the two chapters most likely to feel like opposites of each other, because holding both at once is where most of the real, lasting change actually happens. The upward-drifting comparisons — the trajectory check, the reference group that keeps relocating, the milestone clock, the sibling scoreboard, the professional peer trap, the curated sample, the mismatched decade — all pull in the same direction, making you feel behind a standard that was never fixed to begin with. The downward comparison pulls the opposite way, offering relief instead of anxiety, complacency instead of urgency. It would be easy to read these as two separate problems requiring two separate fixes. They aren't. They're the same instinct, running in two directions depending on which comparison happens to be available at a given moment — which means the actual skill this book has been building, chapter after chapter, isn't "compare upward less" or "compare downward less." It's noticing the comparison at all, regardless of which direction it's currently pulling, and asking the same honest question of it every time: is this actually a fair measure of my own life, or just the nearest one.

This book carries no product, no account type, no allocation strategy, because none of those things were ever the actual subject. The actual subject, in every chapter, was a question of where your standard for "enough," "on track," or "behind" actually comes from — and whether the person, group, or era supplying that standard was ever a fair one to measure against in the first place. That's not a question a financial instrument can answer for you, however well designed. It's a question only you can ask, chapter by chapter, comparison by comparison, for the rest of a financial life that was always, underneath every scoreboard this book has named, entirely your own to evaluate on its own terms.

It's worth returning, one last time, to the question that ran quietly underneath every chapter in this book: is the person, group, or number I'm measuring against actually a fair comparison for the life I'm actually living? Most of the time, examined honestly, the answer turns out to be no — not because comparison itself is a mistake, but because the specific comparison running in any given moment was almost never chosen deliberately enough to deserve the authority it's been quietly given. A friend group assembled by accident of geography. A reference group that drifted upward the moment you stopped watching it. A milestone borrowed from a source nobody can name. A sibling relationship carrying a scoreboard from childhood. A curated sample built by an algorithm with no interest in showing you anything representative. None of these were ever built to be fair measuring sticks. They became measuring sticks anyway, simply by being close enough, visible enough, and persistent enough to fill the space where a genuinely chosen standard should have been.

There is a broader truth worth carrying forward past this specific book, into whatever other parts of life this instinct touches beyond money: the comparison instinct doesn't confine itself to bank balances. It runs on career, on parenting, on health, on nearly every domain where a fixed, objective standard is hard to come by and a nearby person is easy to find instead. If the work of this book helps you catch the comparison instinct operating in your financial life — naming the reference group, tracing the milestone, separating the relief from the evidence — there's a real chance it will teach you something useful about every other domain where the same instinct has been quietly setting terms you never consented to.

For most readers, the work ahead isn't dramatic. It's a reference group named out loud instead of left to run silently. A goal revisited on its own numbers instead of someone else's update. A pause of a week before a comparison-driven decision gets made permanent. A sentence, practiced enough times to become automatic, that interrupts the calculation before it finishes running: *that's information about their life, not a verdict on mine.* None of these moments will feel dramatic when they happen. That's exactly how you'll know they're working — because the scoreboard this book describes was never dramatic either. It built itself in ordinary moments, one comparison at a time, and it will come apart the same way.

There's one last thing worth saying, because it's easy to lose track of across nine chapters of mechanism and cost: none of this makes you unusual, weak, or particularly susceptible compared to anyone else. Every person interviewed in the course of building this book — freelancers, salaried professionals, retirees, people just starting out — recognized at least one of these nine rooms almost immediately, usually with a small, rueful laugh of recognition rather than surprise. That near-universal recognition is itself the point. This isn't a character flaw a smaller number of unusually insecure people happen to carry. It's a standard-issue feature of a mind built, over a very long evolutionary history, to care intensely about relative standing — now running, mostly unexamined, on a domain that history never quite prepared it for.

You do not need anyone's permission to stop measuring your life against a scoreboard you never agreed to keep. You only need to notice, the next time the calculation starts running, that it's running at all.

Notes & Further Reading

The psychological concepts referenced throughout this book are drawn from established research in social psychology, behavioral economics, developmental psychology, and labor economics. Readers interested in the underlying research may find the following starting points useful. As with any popular treatment of academic research, readers seeking deeper or more technical coverage should consult the primary sources and current peer-reviewed literature directly, rather than relying on this book's necessarily brief summaries.

Social comparison theory: Leon Festinger's original 1954 paper "A Theory of Social Comparison Processes," published in *Human Relations*, remains the foundational text for understanding how people evaluate themselves relative to others' judgments and standards, and underlies nearly every chapter in this book.

Reference group theory: Sociologist Robert K. Merton's work on reference groups, particularly as developed in *Social Theory and Social Structure* (1968), is the foundational framework for understanding how people select comparison groups, and how those groups need not be personally known to exert real psychological influence.

Loss aversion, prospect theory, and reference points: Daniel Kahneman and Amos Tversky's foundational 1979 paper "Prospect Theory: An Analysis of Decision under Risk," published in *Econometrica*, and Kahneman's later synthesis in *Thinking, Fast and Slow* (2011), are the primary references for reference-point shifts, loss aversion, and the availability heuristic discussed across several chapters.

Impression management and self-presentation: Erving Goffman's *The Presentation of Self in Everyday Life* (1959) is the foundational text for the framework describing how people selectively present favorable information about themselves, referenced throughout this book's discussion of curated and incomplete comparison samples.

Self-discrepancy theory: Psychologist E. Tory Higgins's foundational research, including "Self-Discrepancy: A Theory Relating Self and Affect," published in *Psychological Review*

(1987), is the primary reference for the distinction between "ought" and "ideal" selves discussed in the chapters on trajectory and milestone comparison.

The hedonic treadmill: Philip Brickman and Donald T. Campbell's foundational 1971 essay "Hedonic Relativism and Planning the Good Society" introduced the concept later developed extensively in subjective well-being research, referenced in the discussion of reference group drift.

Positional goods: Economist Fred Hirsch's *Social Limits to Growth* (1976) introduced the concept of positional goods, later extended substantially by economist Robert H. Frank in works including *Luxury Fever* (1999) and *Falling Behind: How Rising Inequality Harms the Middle Class* (2007).

Benign and malicious envy: Niels van de Ven, Marcel Zeelenberg, and Rik Pieters's research, including "Leveling Up and Down: The Experiences of Benign and Malicious Envy," published in *Emotion* (2009), is the primary reference for the distinction discussed in the chapter on return-chasing.

Informational cascades: Sushil Bikhchandani, David Hirshleifer, and Ivo Welch's foundational paper "A Theory of Fads, Fashion, Custom, and Cultural Change as Informational Cascades," published in the *Journal of Political Economy* (1992), is the primary reference for how individual decisions can be swept along by observed group behavior under uncertainty.

Social proof: Robert Cialdini's *Influence: The Psychology of Persuasion* is the widely cited synthesis of research on social proof as a driver of behavior, particularly under conditions of uncertainty.

Social norms and normative convergence: Muzafer Sherif's foundational research using the autokinetic effect, published in *The Psychology of Social Norms* (1936), remains the classic demonstration of how shared standards form and persist even without an objective basis, referenced in the discussion of milestone numbers.

The curse of knowledge: Colin Camerer, George Loewenstein, and Martin Weber's "The Curse of Knowledge in

Economic Settings: An Experimental Analysis," published in the *Journal of Political Economy* (1989), is the primary reference for how absorbed information resists later revision.

Family systems theory: Psychiatrist Murray Bowen's foundational work on family systems, including the framework later compiled in *Family Therapy in Clinical Practice* (1978), underlies the discussion of sibling roles and family comparison dynamics.

Differential parental treatment: The body of developmental psychology research on differential treatment of siblings, including foundational work summarized by researchers such as Judy Dunn and Robert Plomin in *Separate Lives: Why Siblings Are So Different* (1990), documents the gap between parents' intentions and children's perceptions.

Equity theory: J. Stacy Adams's foundational work on equity theory, including "Toward an Understanding of Inequity," published in the *Journal of Abnormal and Social Psychology* (1963), is the primary reference for the input-outcome fairness comparisons discussed in the chapters on inheritance and professional compensation.

Downward comparison theory: Thomas Ashby Wills's foundational 1981 paper "Downward Comparison Principles in Social Psychology," published in *Psychological Bulletin*, is the primary reference for the mechanism discussed in the chapter on downward comparison and complacency.

Self-affirmation theory: Claude Steele's foundational work, including "The Psychology of Self-Affirmation: Sustaining the Integrity of the Self," published in *Advances in Experimental Social Psychology* (1988), is referenced in the discussion of how downward comparison can reduce motivation to address real problems.

Relative income and well-being: Economist Erzo F.P. Luttmer's research, including "Neighbors as Negatives: Relative Earnings and Well-Being," published in the *Quarterly Journal of Economics* (2005), is the primary empirical reference for the effect of peer and neighbor income on subjective well-being, independent of absolute income.

Mere exposure effect: Psychologist Robert Zajonc's foundational research, including "Attitudinal Effects of Mere Exposure," published in the *Journal of Personality and Social Psychology* (1968), is the primary reference for how repeated exposure shifts baseline familiarity and perceived normalcy.

Just-world hypothesis: Social psychologist Melvin J. Lerner's foundational research, including *The Belief in a Just World: A Fundamental Delusion* (1980), is the primary reference for the tendency to attribute outcomes to deservingness rather than structural or circumstantial factors, referenced in the discussion of cross-generational comparison.

Cohort and scarring effects in labor economics: The body of labor economics research documenting persistent earnings effects for workers who enter the labor market during recessions includes foundational work by economists including Lisa Kahn, whose research on the long-term effects of graduating into a weak labor market is a frequently cited reference point in this literature.

Easterlin paradox and relative income: Economist Richard Easterlin's foundational research, including "Does Economic Growth Improve the Human Lot?" (1974), established the framework for understanding life satisfaction relative to income as a comparative, rather than purely absolute, phenomenon.

This book takes psychological concepts and research findings as its foundation, credited above, while every scenario, case study, and individual described in these pages is anonymized and archetypal — a composite drawn from common patterns rather than any single identifiable person. No named individual's story appears in this book.

About This Book

The Comparison Instinct is part of the Money Instinct library — a series of short books examining the wired-in psychological patterns that shape how people relate to money, not as a matter of discipline or willpower, but as a matter of instinct: fast, automatic, and usually invisible until it's named. Each book in the library takes one distinct pattern and follows it into the rooms where it actually lives — a dinner table, a shower, a dinner-table estate conversation years later — rather than treating money psychology as an abstract subject to be studied from a distance.

This particular volume sits alongside others in the library that examine different, distinct financial patterns — the one-time distortion of a single anchoring number, the display purchases made for an audience that isn't really watching, the quiet architecture of control inside a shared account — each chosen because it describes a genuinely separate psychological mechanism rather than a relabeled version of a pattern already covered elsewhere. *The Comparison Instinct* is specifically about an ongoing, standing habit: the ordinary, continuous act of measuring your own financial life against other people's, whether or not a single purchase or a single visible decision ever results from it.

This book carries no financial advice, no investment strategy, and no product recommendation. It is not a substitute for financial planning, tax guidance, or professional advice specific to your own circumstances, and nothing in these pages should be read as a recommendation regarding any specific investment, account, or financial product. If anything in this book has stirred up a level of financial anxiety or distress beyond ordinary comparison, please consider speaking with a qualified financial professional or, where the distress feels more emotional than practical, a licensed counselor familiar with financial anxiety. Naming a pattern is a genuine first step. It is rarely the only one needed.

If this book was useful to you, the most meaningful thing you can do is spend five honest minutes naming your own reference group on paper — not to eliminate it, but to finally see it clearly enough to decide, on purpose, how much authority it actually deserves over your next financial decision. That exercise, more than anything else in these pages, is the actual point. Everything else in this book was simply preparation for the moment you sit down and do it.

Also in the Series

Every book in The Money Instinct library stands on its own — read them in any order. If this one was useful, the library continues:

The Money Instinct

The Secrecy Instinct

The Underearning Instinct

The Shame Instinct

The Panic Instinct

The Merge Instinct

The Ceiling Instinct

The Windfall Instinct

The Control Instinct

The Legacy Instinct

The Enabling Instinct

The Austerity Instinct

The Paralysis Instinct

The Retirement Instinct

The Divorce Instinct

The Enough Instinct

The Overconfidence Instinct

The Vigilance Instinct

The Generosity Instinct